■SCHOLASTIC

Shoe Box Learning Centers

Time & Measurement

by Pamela Chanko

NEW YORK • TORONTO • LONDON • AUCKLAND • SYDNEY

MEXICO CITY • NEW DELHI • HONG KONG • BUENOS AIRES

Teaching *Resources*

For my parents, whose timely inspiration helped immeasurably!

Special thanks to Joan Novelli for her boundless creativity and unwavering support. Thanks also to Peter St. Marie, technical engineer and clockmaker extraordinaire.

Edited by Joan Novelli
Cover design by Maria Lilja
Cover photograph by James Levin/Studio 10
Interior design by Holly Grundon
Interior illustrations by James Graham Hale

ISBN 0-439-53797-5
Copyright © 2005 by Pamela Chanko.
Published by Scholastic Inc.

1 2 3 4 5 6 7 8 9 10 40 12 11 10 09 08 07 06 05

CONTENTS

About This Book

As a teacher, you know the value of using learning centers in your classroom. Learning centers give you the opportunity to circulate among individuals or small groups of students, providing on-the-spot instruction, scaffolding, and guidance tailored to the needs of each child. Learning centers greatly benefit children as well. By allowing them to work independently and make their own discoveries, centers help children take responsibility for their own learning—which, in turn, fosters a love of the learning process itself. Centers also give students the opportunity to practice important classroom skills, such as cooperation, teamwork, and respect for the materials.

Shoe Box Learning Centers: Time & Measurement enables you to quickly and easily create 30 engaging, hands-on learning centers that teach important mathematical concepts in fun and creative ways. The concepts of time and measurement can seem abstract to children, and can therefore be challenging to teach. The activities in this book help make these concepts concrete for children as they play games, make discoveries, and even create their own learning materials. Just some of the activities you'll find are:

- fun kits for children to create their own clocks

- a do-it-yourself clip-on time line

- a calendar puzzle

- a year-by-year penny parade

- a frog-jumping measurement contest

- an interactive mini-book

- time and measurement games based on favorite stories and rhymes

- and much more!

The centers come together quickly with labels, directions, and reproducible pages included in this book. Other shoe box center materials are inexpensive or readily available in your classroom or home. The materials for each center fit neatly inside a shoe box, allowing you to assemble them ahead of time, store them conveniently, and pull them out as needed. With a shoe box, a copier, and a few additional materials, a wealth of exciting, independent activities are at your fingertips!

TIP

To help students get the most out of using the centers, model the activities before inviting children to try them on their own.

Setting Up Shoe Box Learning Centers

This book is divided into two sections of 15 centers each: Time (pages 9–43) and Measurement (pages 44–78). The easy-to-follow organization allows you to choose the activities you want to use and set them up in a snap. For each center, you'll find:

- **Title and Directions:** The title becomes the shoe box label. Simply copy it onto colored paper or have children decorate it. Glue the label to one end of the box for easy storage and retrieval. Glue a copy of the student directions to the inside of the box lid.

- **Materials:** Check here to find out which items you'll need for each center. Simply gather the materials and place them in the box.

- **Shoe Box Setup:** Here you'll find simple directions for assembling each center. In most cases, all you'll need to do is gather materials and make copies of the reproducibles.

- **Tips:** These ideas include activity variations and extensions as well as helpful hints for making the most of children's learning experiences.

- **Reproducible Pages:** The reproducible pages (record sheets, patterns, game boards, awards, mini-books, and more) for each center immediately follow the Directions page, making them easy to locate and allowing you to see the whole shoe box setup at a glance.

Meeting the Math Standards

The activities in this book are designed to help you meet the NCTM standards in your classroom. The standards set forth in the NCTM Measurement strand state that classroom instruction should enable students to:

- recognize the attributes of length, volume, weight, area, and time

- compare and order objects according to these attributes

- understand how to measure using nonstandard and standard units

- select an appropriate unit and tool for the attribute being measured

- use tools to measure

- develop common referents for measures to make comparisons and estimates

Each of these standards is covered throughout the book, and each shoe box activity supports several. The chart on page 8 identifies specific target skills for each activity. In addition to helping you meet the content standard for measurement, the shoe box centers in this book support the process standards—including problem-solving, reasoning and proof, communication, connections, and representation.

Reinforcing and Assessing Student Learning

One of the greatest benefits of using centers in math is that they provide teachers with the opportunity to work with small groups or individuals on the concepts and skills being taught in the classroom. The center setup makes it easy to review concepts and provide individual assistance as needed. To record students' progress as they move through centers, you may want to create assessment files. To do so, provide a pocket folder for each student. In the first pocket, place a checklist of all the centers so that students can keep track of those they have completed. (See page 7 for a reproducible Shoe Box Learning Centers Checklist.) In the second, have students store completed record sheets for review. For activities that do not require record sheets, sticky notes work well as an assessment tool. Observe students as they work with a shoe box center, and ask related questions. Jot comments on sticky notes, and record the child's name, the date, and the shoe box center name. Keep these on a separate sheet of paper in the pocket folder for easy reference. In addition, comments for any center can be recorded on the checklist. Use these assessments to guide students' work with the centers. Encourage students to revisit those centers in which they show a need for more practice.

Shoe Box Learning Centers Checklist

Name_____

Shoe Box Learning Center	Date	Comments
Clockmaker Faces		
Hickory, Dickory, Spin the Clock		
Gimme Fives		
Bedtime Bears		
Buzz		
Make My Day		
Dragon's Day		
Time Line Tales		
Happy Birthday to Me		
Penny Parade		
Yesterday, Today, Tomorrow		
It's a Toss-Up		
Egg Timer Estimations		
Count on the Calendar		
Calendar Cutups		
One-Inch Art		
Inchworm, Inchworm		
To Grandmother's House We Go		
Jump, Frog, Jump!		
Max's Measurement Diner		
Growing a Garden		
Pet Show		
Park It!		
The Great Gack Olympics		
Pizza, Please!		
Build a Skyline		
To Market, to Market		
Three Bears Fill Their Bowls		
The Old Woman Who Lived in a Shoe		
Measuring Mini-Books		

Meeting the Math Standards

Shoe Box Learning Center	Understand Measurable Attributes							Apply Techniques and Formulas				
	recognize length	recognize volume	recognize weight	recognize area	recognize time	compare/order objects	use nonstandard/standard units	select appropriate unit/tool	use multiple copies of units	use repetition of single unit	use tools to measure	make comparisons/estimates
Clockmaker Faces					X		X	X			X	
Hickory, Dickory, Spin the Clock					X		X					
Gimme Fives					X		X	X			X	
Bedtime Bears					X		X					X
Buzz					X		X	X			X	
Make My Day					X	X						
Dragon's Day					X	X	X					
Time Line Tales					X	X	X					
Happy Birthday to Me					X	X				X		
Penny Parade					X	X						X
Yesterday, Today, Tomorrow					X	X						X
It's a Toss-Up					X		X	X			X	X
Egg Timer Estimations					X		X	X				X
Count on the Calendar					X		X				X	
Calendar Cutups					X	X	X					
One-Inch Art	X			X			X					
Inchworm, Inchworm	X						X	X	X		X	X
To Grandmother's House We Go	X						X	X	X		X	X
Jump, Frog, Jump!	X						X	X		X	X	X
Max's Measurement Diner	X						X	X			X	
Growing a Garden	X						X	X	X		X	X
Pet Show	X					X	X	X			X	X
Park It!	X			X			X	X			X	
The Great Gack Olympics	X						X	X		X	X	X
Pizza, Please!				X			X	X	X		X	X
Build a Skyline	X			X		X	X					X
To Market, to Market			X				X		X		X	X
Three Bears Fill Their Bowls		X					X	X			X	X
The Old Woman Who Lived in a Shoe		X					X	X	X		X	X
Measuring Mini-Books	X	X	X		X		X					

Shoe Box Learning Centers: Time & Measurement • Scholastic Teaching Resources

Clockmaker Faces

Children become clockmakers as they create self-portrait clock faces.

Materials

- shoe box
- box label
- student directions
- scissors
- glue
- clock patterns (page 10)
- paper fasteners
- pencils
- crayons
- yarn (various colors)

Shoe Box Setup

Copy the clock patterns onto card stock and cut out the pieces. To create the clocks, pass a paper fastener through the base of each hand and then through the center of the clock. Place the clocks, glue, pencils, crayons, and yarn in the shoe box. Glue the label to one end of the box and the student directions to the inside of the lid. Set aside an eye-level bulletin board or wall space for children to display their completed clocks.

TIP Explain to children that the surface of a clock is called a face. Invite children to share their ideas about how they think it got that name. Let children compare their clock faces and tell how they are alike and different. For time-telling practice, have children set their clocks to the current time at various points throughout the day.

Reading an Analog Clock

Clockmaker Faces

Directions

(1) Write the numbers 1 through 12 in the correct spaces on a clock face.

(2) Color in the clock face to look like you. Draw eyes and a mouth, and glue yarn for hair.

(3) Set the clock to match the time on the classroom clock.

(4) Practice setting the clock for different times of day.

Clockmaker Faces

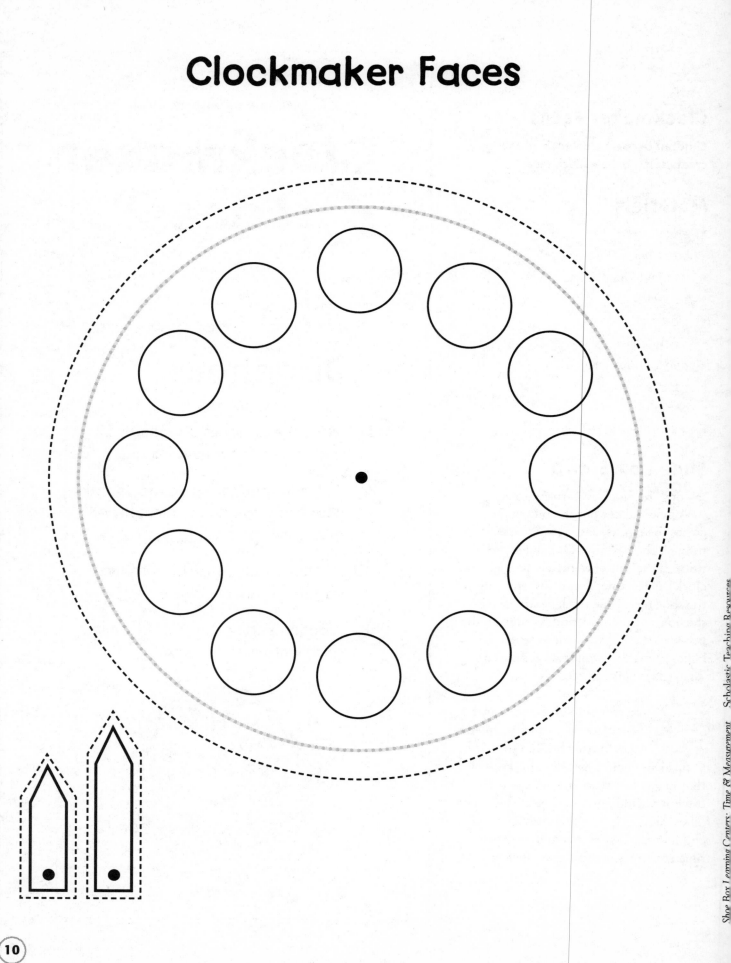

Shoe Box Learning Centers: Time & Measurement Scholastic Teaching Resources

Hickory, Dickory, Spin the Clock

Children practice telling time as they help the mouse run up the clock!

Materials

- shoe box
- box label
- student directions
- scissors
- glue
- game board (page 12)
- spinner and game markers (page 13)
- paper clip
- paper fastener

Shoe Box Setup

Copy the game board, spinner, and game markers onto card stock. To set up the spinner, pass the paper fastener through the paper clip, then through the center of the spinner. Adjust the fastener so that the clip spins easily. Place the game board, spinner, and game markers in the shoe box. Glue the label to one end of the box and the student directions to the inside of the lid.

TIP To create a different game board, use correction fluid to white out the time labels and write in your own. Write times to the hour, repeating a series of five or six different times.

Reading an Analog Clock

Hickory, Dickory, Spin the Clock

Directions
(for 2–4 players)

 1 Each player takes a mouse marker. Place the markers on Start.

2 Take turns spinning the clock. Spin the paper clip and pretend it's the hour hand. Read the time to the closest hour.

3 Move your marker forward to the nearest space with the matching time. If you can't find a time that matches, spin again.

 4 Continue taking turns until one player's mouse reaches the top of the clock.

Hickory, Dickory, Spin the Clock

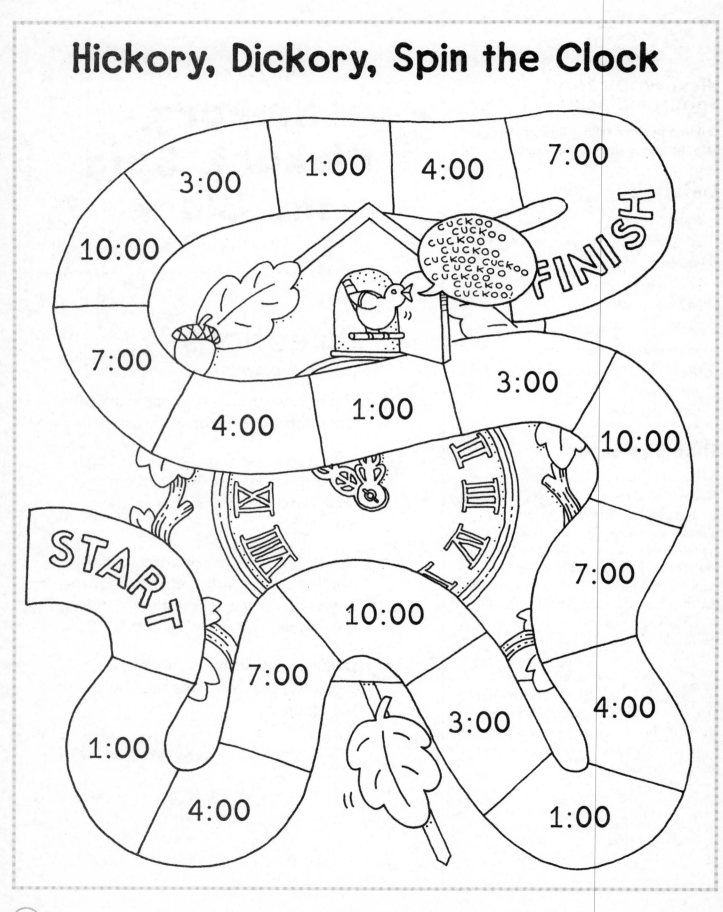

Shoe Box Learning Centers: Time & Measurement   Scholastic Teaching Resources

Hickory, Dickory, Spin the Clock

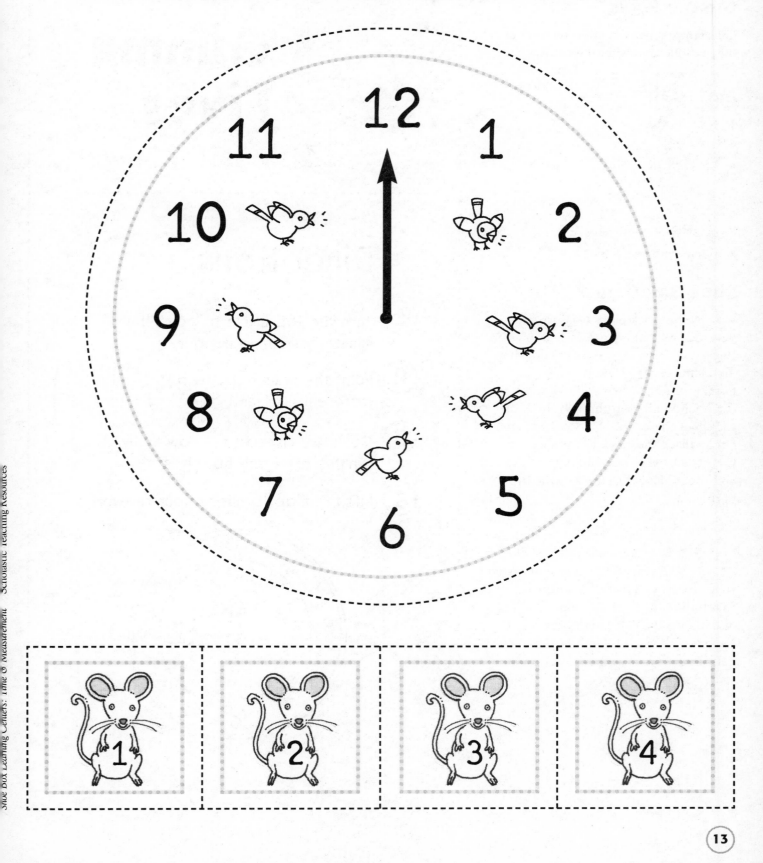

Gimme Fives

Children practice counting by fives as they tell the time after the hour.

Materials

- shoe box
- box label
- student directions
- scissors
- glue
- clock patterns (page 15)
- paper fasteners

Shoe Box Setup

Copy the clock patterns onto card stock. Cut along the dashed lines on the small circle to create a window flap. To complete the clock, pass a paper fastener through the middle of the X on the hour hand, then through the X on the small circle, and the X on the large circle. Place the clock in the shoe box. Glue the label to one end of the shoe box and the student directions to the inside of the lid.

TIP Explain to children that each number on the clock represents a five-minute span of time. Together, practice counting by fives to tell the time after the hour. You might also discuss the placement of the hour hand and show children how it moves between numbers as the minutes pass.

Reading an Analog Clock

Gimme Fives

Directions

1. Turn the top circle to point the minute hand to a number.

2. Point the hour hand to a different number.

3. Count by fives to tell how many minutes after the hour it is.

4. Lift the flap to check your answer.

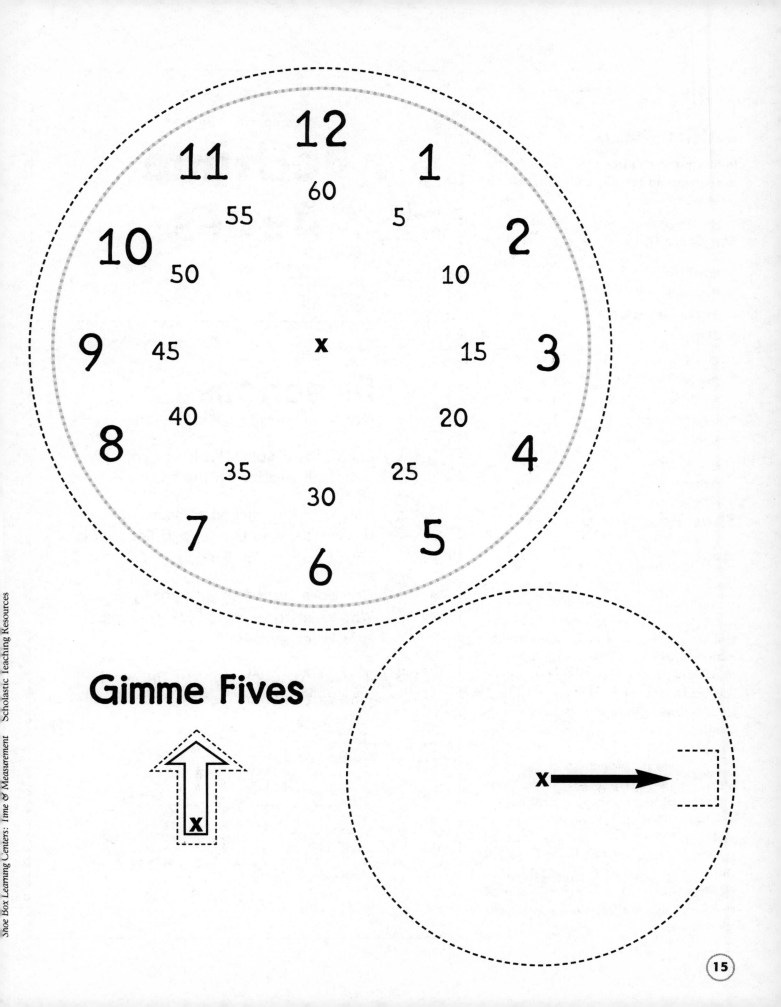

Gimme Fives

Bedtime Bears

In this game, children compare bedtimes over a week to see who can collect the most teddy bears.

Materials

- shoe box
- box label
- student directions
- scissors
- glue
- bedtime board and spinners (page 17)
- counting bears
- paper fasteners
- paper clips
- pencils

Shoe Box Setup

Make copies of the bedtime boards. Copy the spinners onto card stock. Place a paper clip in the center of each spinner and fasten loosely with a paper fastener (so that the clip will spin easily). Collect seven colored counting bears for each game. Place the boards, spinners, bears, and pencils in the shoe box. Glue the label to one end of the box and the student directions to the inside of the lid.

TIP Talk with children about the concept of P.M. before they play the game. Explain that P.M. hours occur from noon until midnight. After 12 P.M., the numbers start over with 1. The higher the number, the later the hour. Also explain that if children spin a 5 on the minutes spinner, they write that as 05 to show the number of minutes.

Bedtime Bears

Directions
(for 2 players)

1 Each player spins the hours spinner. Write the number on the first line.

2 Now spin the minutes spinner. Write the numbers on the second line. Read your bedtime for Sunday.

3 Compare bedtimes with your partner. Who went to bed earlier? That player gets a teddy bear.

4 Repeat for each night of the week. Who got the most teddy bears in all?

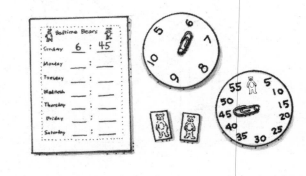

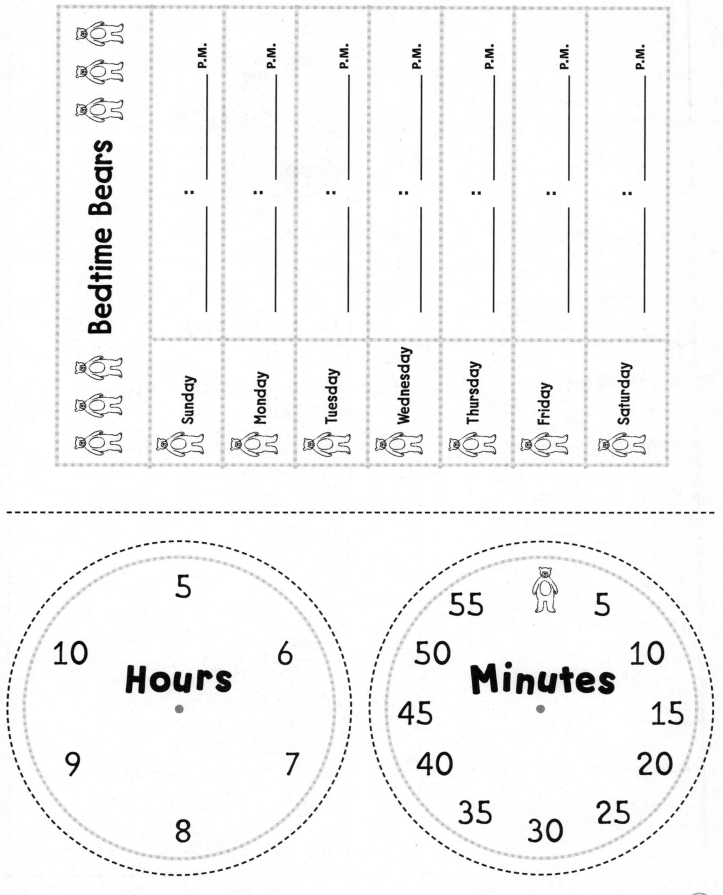

Bedtime Bears

Sunday	: _____ P.M.
Monday	: _____ P.M.
Tuesday	: _____ P.M.
Wednesday	: _____ P.M.
Thursday	: _____ P.M.
Friday	: _____ P.M.
Saturday	: _____ P.M.

Hours

5 6 7 8 9 10

Minutes

55 5 50 10 45 15 40 20 35 30 25

Buzz

Children practice setting the "alarm" on a digital clock they create themselves.

Materials

- shoe box
- box label
- student directions
- scissors
- glue
- alarm clock (page 19)
- pull-through strips (page 19)
- resealable plastic bags

Shoe Box Setup

Copy the clock face and pull-through strips onto card stock and cut them out. Cut along the dashed lines on the alarm clock to create five pull-through windows. For each clock, thread the strips through as follows: Thread strip 1 (word strip) through top slit of the first window and down through bottom slit. Thread strip 2 (with numbers 0–1) through the second window; strip 3 (0–9) through the third window; strip 4 (0–5) through the fourth window; and strip 5 (0–9) through the fifth window. Place the clocks in the shoe box. Glue the label to one end of the box and the student directions to the inside of the lid.

TIP You can expand this activity by creating additional strips for the "Time to…" window. Simply write new activities that children can set their alarms for on a strip of paper. Have children replace the original strip in the first window of their clock with a new one.

Reading a Digital Clock

Buzz

Directions

1. Pull on the first strip to choose an activity.

2. What time do you this activity? Set the alarm on your clock to help you remember. Pull the number strips to show the time you do the activity. Buzz!

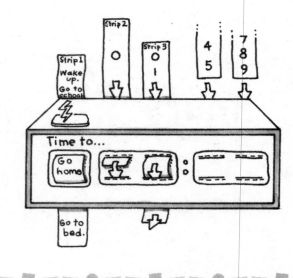

Shoe Box Learning Centers: Time & Measurement   Scholastic Teaching Resources

Buzz

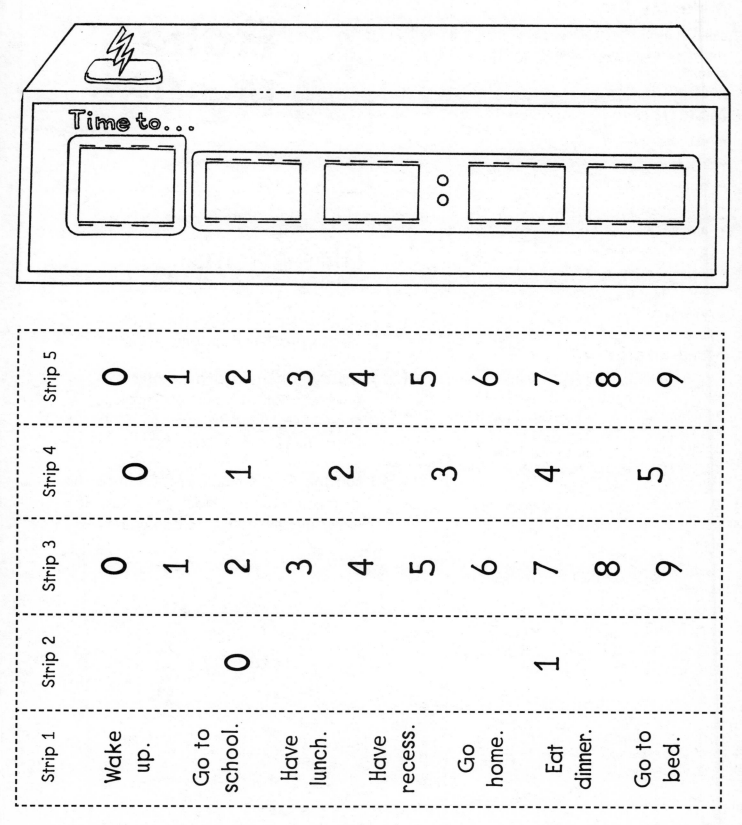

Time to...

Strip 1	Strip 2	Strip 3	Strip 4	Strip 5
Wake up.	0	0	0	0
Go to school.		1	1	1
Have lunch.		2	2	2
Have recess.		3	3	3
Go home.		4	4	4
Eat dinner.	1	5	5	5
Go to bed.		6		6
		7		7
		8		8
		9		9

Sequencing Time

Make My Day

Children make a flip book to create stories about morning, afternoon, and evening activities.

Materials

- shoe box
- box label
- student directions
- scissors
- glue
- flip book template (page 21)
- paper fasteners
- crayons
- pencils

Shoe Box Setup

Make three or more copies of the template for each book. Line up the sheets and insert paper fasteners through the circles. Cut along the dashed lines to separate the pages of the flip book. Leave the solid lines intact. Place the flip books, crayons, and pencils in the shoe box. Glue the label to one end of the box and the student directions to the inside of the lid.

TIP To take the lesson on time further, modify the flip book template to include clock faces. Children can fill in the hands on the clocks to show the times they do each activity.

Sequencing Time

Make My Day

Directions

1. Think of activities you do in the morning, afternoon, and evening.

2. Write words and draw pictures in each section of your flip book to show things you do at each of those times.

3. Flip the pages back and forth to tell different stories about your day. How many different stories can you make?

Make My Day

Name _____ Date _____

In the morning I . . .

_____

_____

_____

Draw a picture.

In the afternoon I . . .

_____

_____

_____

Draw a picture.

In the evening I . . .

_____

_____

_____

Draw a picture.

Shoe Box Learning Centers: Time & Measurement   Scholastic Teaching Resources

Dragon's Day

Children practice reading time as they sequence the order of events in a dragon's day.

Materials

- shoe box
- box label
- student directions
- scissors
- glue
- time sequence cards (pages 23–24)
- rubber bands

Shoe Box Setup

Copy the picture cards onto card stock and cut them apart. Shuffle each set of cards and secure with a rubber band. Place the cards in the shoe box. Glue the label to one end of the box and the student directions to the inside of the lid.

TIP Discuss A.M. and P.M. with children before doing this activity. You can also customize decks of cards for students at different levels. For a simpler sequencing activity, use only the cards with hour readings. As children become more proficient, add in the half hours. Children can also sort the cards into A.M. and P.M. piles, or by morning, afternoon, and evening. For an extra challenge, ask children to sequence the cards in reverse order.

Sequencing Time

Dragon's Day

Directions

1. Shuffle the cards and place them faceup on a table.

2. Look at each picture. Tell what Dragon is doing. Read the time.

3. Put the pictures in order. Tell the story of Dragon's day.

Shoe Box Learning Centers: Time & Measurement   Scholastic Teaching Resources

Dragon's Day

7:30 A.M.

8:00 A.M.

8:30 A.M.

9:00 A.M.

9:30 A.M.

10:00 A.M.

10:30 A.M.

11:00 A.M.

11:30 A.M.

12:00 P.M.

12:30 P.M.

1:00 P.M.

Dragon's Day

1:30 P.M.

2:00 P.M.

2:30 P.M.

3:00 P.M.

3:30 P.M.

4:00 P.M.

4:30 P.M.

5:00 P.M.

5:30 P.M.

6:00 P.M.

6:30 P.M.

7:00 P.M.

Shoe Box Learning Centers: Time & Measurement   Scholastic Teaching Resources

Time Line Tales

Children clip clothespins on a yarn clothesline to make time lines that sequence events in their day.

Materials

- shoe box
- box label
- student directions
- scissors
- glue
- time line cards (page 26)
- yarn
- clothespins
- crayons
- pencils
- paper

Shoe Box Setup

Copy the time line cards onto card stock and cut them apart. For each time line, cut a length of yarn (about 36 inches) and attach the number of clothespins you'd like to use. Place the cards, time line strings, clothespins, crayons, pencils, and paper in the shoe box. Glue the label to one end of the box and the student directions to the inside of the lid.

TIP For a simpler time line, include four cards with different times and attach four clothespins to the yarn. Use copies of the blank time line card to include more times (such as half hours), or have students designate their own times to make new time lines. As a variation, invite students to create a time line to show what would happen in a perfect day.

Sequencing Time

Time Line Tales

Directions

1. Choose a card. Read the clock.

2. Draw a picture to show what happens in your day at that time.

3. Repeat for each card.

4. Use a clothespin to attach each card and picture in order to the clothesline.

5. Use the time line to tell a story about your day.

Time Line Tales

8:00 A.M.

9:00 A.M.

10:00 A.M.

11:00 A.M.

12:00 P.M.

1:00 P.M.

2:00 P.M.

3:00 P.M.

4:00 P.M.

5:00 P.M.

6:00 P.M.

_____ : _____ P.M.

Shoe Box Learning Centers: Time & Measurement Scholastic Teaching Resources

Happy Birthday to Me

Children measure years with candles as they sequence their own birthday cakes.

Materials

- shoe box
- box label
- student directions
- scissors
- glue
- cake patterns (page 28)
- birthday candle patterns (page 29)
- resealable plastic bags
- crayons

Shoe Box Setup

Make multiple copies of the cake and candle patterns. Cut out the cakes and candles. Make sets of eight cakes each, labeling them as follows: 1 year old, 2 years old, 3 years old, 4 years old, 5 years old, 6 years old, 7 years old, and 8 years old. Place each set of cakes and candles in a bag. Place the glue, bags, and crayons in the shoe box. Glue the label to one end of the box and the student directions to the inside of the lid.

TIP To add a writing component and make a keepsake time line, have children glue their birthday cakes in order on a long sheet of paper. Have them write or dictate something about each year of their lives.

Happy Birthday to Me

Directions

1. Choose a set of birthday cakes and candles.

2. Draw a picture on each cake to show what you looked like at that age.

3. Glue candles on each cake to show how many years old you were.

4. Put your birthday cakes in order. How did you change each year?

Happy Birthday to Me

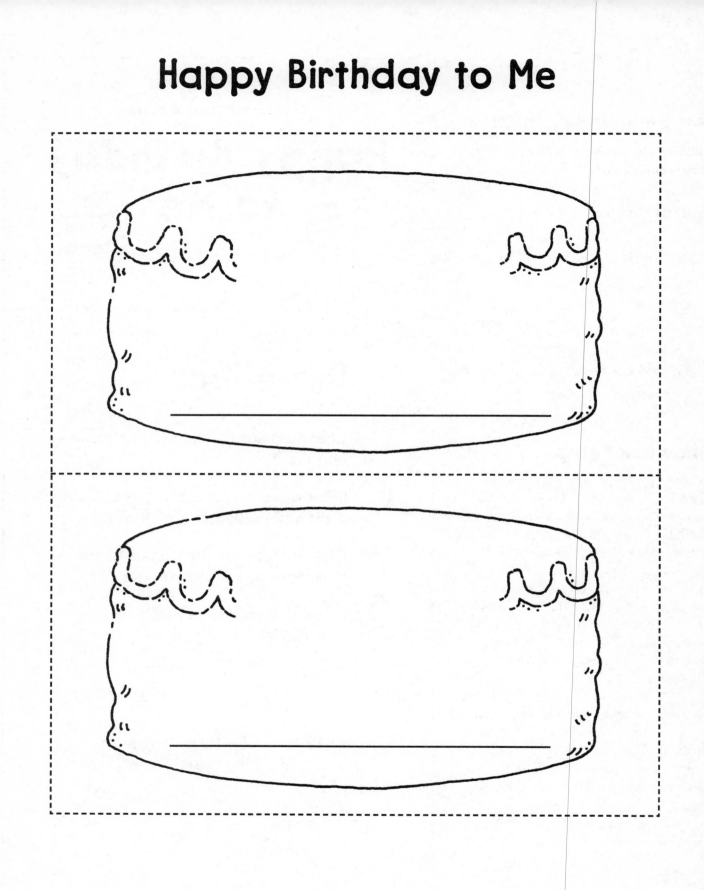

Shoe Box Learning Centers: Time & Measurement   Scholastic Teaching Resources

Happy Birthday to Me

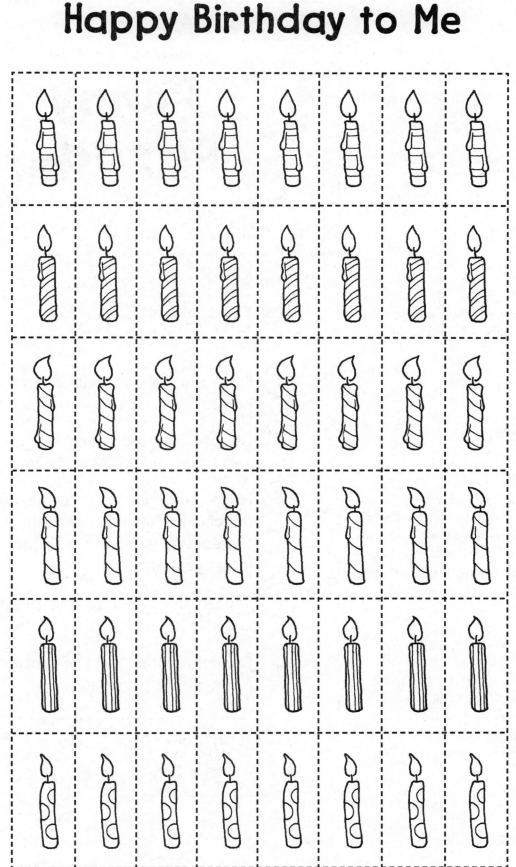

Penny Parade

Children sequence time by years as they arrange pennies in a parade.

Materials

- shoe box
- box label
- student directions
- scissors
- glue
- parade strips (page 31)
- sets of 10 pennies (each set to represent 10 different years)
- resealable plastic bags
- paper
- pencils

Shoe Box Setup

Copy the parade strips onto card stock. Tape the strips together to form one long parade. Place each set of 10 pennies in a separate bag. Include a range of years in each set. Place the parade strips, penny bags, paper, and pencils in the shoe box. Glue the label to one end of the box and the student directions to the inside of the lid.

 TIP For a shorter penny parade, use one strip. For a greater challenge, tape three or more strips together to make a longer parade. You can also challenge students to sequence the pennies in reverse order, starting with the latest year and ending with the earliest.

Sequencing Time in Years

Penny Parade

Directions

1. Place the parade strip in front of you.

2. Choose a bag of pennies. Read the year on each penny.

3. Place the pennies on the parade marchers in order. Start with the earliest year. End with the latest year.

4. Record the dates on your pennies in order.

5. Choose another bag of pennies and make a new parade.

Shoe Box Learning Centers: Time & Measurement Scholastic Teaching Resources

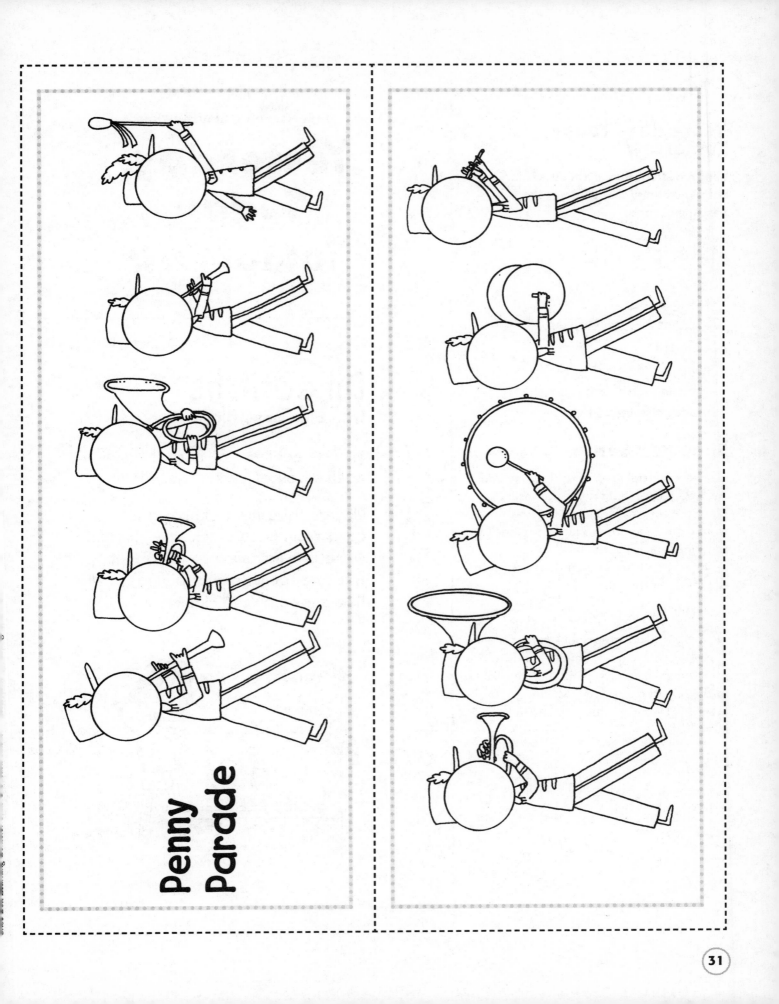

Penny
Parade

Yesterday, Today, Tomorrow

Children strengthen math vocabulary with an activity that explores the passage of time.

Materials

- shoe box
- box label
- student directions
- scissors
- glue
- time and word cards (page 33)
- resealable plastic bags

Shoe Box Setup

Make multiple copies of the time and word cards. Cut apart the cards. Place the time cards in one bag and the word cards in another. Place the cards in the shoe box. Glue the label to one end of the box and the student directions to the inside of the lid.

TIP **F**or practice telling time, substitute clock cards for the time cards. Draw in hands to show times that correspond to activities in the school day, such as Morning Meeting, Literacy Time, Lunch, and Dismissal.

Understanding Elapsed Time

Yesterday, Today, Tomorrow

Directions
(for 2 or more players)

(1) Shuffle each set of cards. Place each stack of cards facedown.

(2) Players take turns choosing a card from each stack. Use the time word in a sentence to tell about what happens (or happened) at the time shown on the clock.

Yesterday, Today, Tomorrow

Time Card __7__ : __00__ A.M.	Time Card __9__ : __00__ A.M.	Time Card __11__ : __00__ A.M.
Time Card __12__ : __00__ P.M.	Time Card __3__ : __00__ P.M.	Time Card __7__ : __00__ P.M.
Yesterday	Today	Tomorrow
Yesterday	Today	Tomorrow

It's a Toss-Up

Children keep track of time as they race to complete a variety of activities.

Materials

- shoe box
- box label
- student directions
- scissors
- glue
- score sheet (page 35)
- game cubes (page 36)
- clock or timer
- pencils

Shoe Box Setup

Make several copies of the score sheet. Copy the game cube patterns onto sturdy paper and cut them apart. To assemble the cubes, fold along the solid lines and glue to secure. Set aside the blank cube for later use. (See Tip, below.) Place the score sheets, game cubes, clock or timer, and pencils in the shoe box. Glue the label to one end of the box and the student directions to the inside of the lid.

TIP To create new games, make two copies of the blank cube. Write the activities on one cube and the number of repetitions on the other.

Understanding Elapsed Time

It's a Toss-Up

Directions
(for 2 players)

 The first player tosses the game cubes. Read the activity on one cube. Read the number on the other cube. This is the number of times you will do the activity.

 Have your partner write your start time on the score sheet. Do the activity. Record the finish time. Subtract the start time from the finish time to get the total time.

 The second player repeats steps 1 and 2.

 Players continue tossing the cubes and keeping score until the score sheets are full. Players add up the minutes in the last column. The player with the lowest score wins the game.

Shoe Box Learning Centers: Time & Measurement · Scholastic Teaching Resources

It's a Toss-Up

Name _____ Date _____

Round 1   Start Time   Finish Time   Total Time

_____ : _____   _____ : _____   _____ minutes

Round 2   Start Time   Finish Time   Total Time

_____ : _____   _____ : _____   _____ minutes

Round 3   Start Time   Finish Time   Total Time

_____ : _____   _____ : _____   _____ minutes

Round 4   Start Time   Finish Time   Total Time

_____ : _____   _____ : _____   _____ minutes

Round 5   Start Time   Finish Time   Total Time

_____ : _____   _____ : _____   _____ minutes

Game Cubes

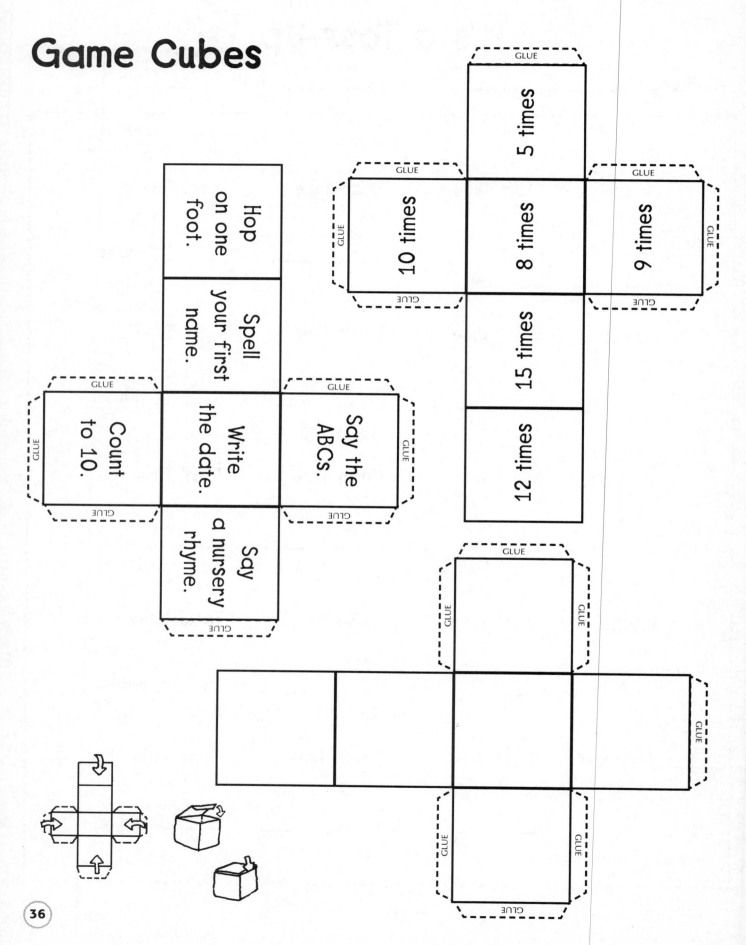

Cube 1 (activity cube):
- Hop on one foot.
- Spell your first name.
- Write the date.
- Say a nursery rhyme.
- Say the ABCs.
- Count to 10.

Cube 2 (times cube):
- 5 times
- 10 times
- 8 times
- 9 times
- 15 times
- 12 times

Shoe Box Learning Centers: Time & Measurement   Scholastic Teaching Resources

Egg Timer Estimations

Children see how much they can do before the sand runs out on an egg timer.

Materials

- shoe box
- box label
- student directions
- scissors
- glue
- record sheet (page 38)
- hourglass-style egg timer (1 minute)
- activity materials (stackable blocks, paper clips, beads, yarn, paper, hole punch, crayons, inkpad, stamper)
- paper
- pencils
- analog clock with second hand

Shoe Box Setup

Make several copies of the record sheet. (Adjust the times listed in the last section on the record sheet as necessary to include a time that matches the egg timer students will use.) Place the record sheets, timer, activity materials, paper, pencils, and clock in the shoe box. Glue the label to one end of the box and the student directions to the inside of the lid.

TIP You can create new games by replacing the activities in the first column with your own. You might like to try silly activities, such as "How many jumping jacks can you do?" or "How many times can you sing 'Happy Birthday' all the way through?"

Understanding Elapsed Time

Egg Timer Estimations

Directions

(1) Make sure all the sand is on one end of the timer. Read the first question.

(2) Guess how much you can do before the sand runs out. Write your guess.

(3) Turn over the timer and do the activity. Stop when all the sand has poured through the timer. Write the number.

(4) Repeat with each activity.

(5) Guess how long it takes for the sand to run through the timer. Circle your guess. Turn over the timer and watch the clock. Circle the time.

Egg Timer Estimations

Name _____ Date _____

	Task	My Guess	Actual Number
	How many beads can you string?		
	How many holes can you punch?		
	How many blocks can you stack?		
	How many clips can you chain?		
	How many smiley faces can you draw?		
	How many stamps can you stamp?		
	How long does it take for all the sand to go through the timer?	1 minute 3 minutes 5 minutes	1 minute 3 minutes 5 minutes

Shoe Box Learning Centers: Time & Measurement Scholastic Teaching Resources

Count on the Calendar

A calendar becomes a game board as children learn about days, weeks, and months.

Materials

- shoe box
- box label
- student directions
- scissors
- glue
- calendar grid (page 40)
- game cards (page 41)
- number cube
- game markers (different shapes or colors)

Shoe Box Setup

Copy the calendar grid and game cards onto card stock. To complete the game board, write the name of the current month and fill in the numerals in the appropriate spaces. If there are directions on the space for the last day of the month, white them out. Cut out the game cards. Place the calendar, game cards, number cube, and game markers in the shoe box. Glue the label to one end of the box and the student directions to the inside of the lid.

TIP For a more challenging game, create a game board that covers several months. Simply make extra copies of the calendar grid, fill them in, and tape them together in sequential order.

Reading a Calendar

Count on the Calendar

Directions
(for 2–4 players)

1 Each player takes a game marker. Place all the markers on the first day of the month. Stack the game cards next to the board. Each time a card is used, place it on the bottom of the pile.

2 The first player rolls the number cube and moves ahead that many days on the calendar. The player follows any directions on the space. Then it is the next player's turn.

3 Continue taking turns. The first player to reach the end of the month wins the game.

Month _____

Sunday	Monday	Tuesday	Wednesday	Thursday	Friday	Saturday
Pick a card.		Pick a card.		Trade places with another player.		Pick a card.
	Pick a card.		Pick a card.	It's a special day! Go again!	Pick a card.	
Lose a turn.	Pick a card.		Go back one space.		Pick a card.	Move ahead 2 spaces.
Pick a card.		Pick a card.	It's a special day! Go again!	Pick a card.		Pick a card.
	Trade places with another player.				Go back one space.	
Pick a card.						

Shoe Box Learning Centers: Time & Measurement   Scholastic Teaching Resources

Count on the Calendar

Today's your lucky day! Move ahead 1 whole week.

It's your birthday! Move ahead 3 days.

Oops! You forgot to return your library books. Go back 3 days.

You need to catch up on your homework! Move back 1 day.

You can't wait to visit your grandparents this weekend! Move ahead to the next Saturday.

You missed your music club meeting! Go back to the last Tuesday.

Time flies when you're having fun! Move ahead to tomorrow.

You missed a playdate. Go back to yesterday.

Too much to do in too little time! Move back 1 week.

It's time for a new week at school. Move ahead to the next Monday.

Vacation time goes fast! Move ahead 5 days.

Oh no! You had a cold and missed school. Go back 4 days.

Calendar Cutups

Children practice reading a calendar as they put together a puzzle for different months.

Materials

- shoe box
- box label
- student directions
- scissors
- glue
- calendar template (page 43)
- paper lunch bags

Shoe Box Setup

Make several copies of the calendar template on card stock, two for each month puzzle you'd like to create. Write the name of the month on top and numerals for dates in the appropriate squares. For each puzzle kit, leave one calendar intact and cut the other into pieces (by month, days, and dates). Place the puzzle pieces in a bag and label with the appropriate month. Place the calendar boards and puzzle bags in the shoe box. Glue the label to one end of the box and the student directions to the inside of the lid.

TIP You might like to note special days on the calendar puzzles, such as vacation days, holidays, and children's birthdays. For a more challenging puzzle, provide children with filled-in puzzle pieces and a blank calendar board. Children can use sequencing skills and their knowledge of calendars to put the pieces together on top of the board. Make a calendar available for reference.

Reading a Calendar

Calendar Cutups

Directions

(1) Choose a month. Place the calendar board in front of you.

(2) Choose the bag of puzzle pieces for the same month.

(3) Place each piece on top of the calendar where it belongs.

(4) Try it again with a new month.

Month _____

Sunday	Monday	Tuesday	Wednesday	Thursday	Friday	Saturday

One-Inch Art

Children become familiar with the inch as a unit of measure as they create a colorful, textured collage.

Materials

- shoe box
- box label
- student directions
- scissors
- glue
- one-inch squares of various colors and textures (such as construction paper, foil, tissue paper, gift wrap, wallpaper, and sandpaper)
- construction paper
- resealable plastic bags

Shoe Box Setup

Collect a variety of colored and textured paper. Cut the paper into one-inch squares. Store the squares in the bags. Place the squares, glue, and construction paper in the shoe box. Glue the label to one end of the box and the student directions to the inside of the lid.

TIP For easier cutting, line up sheets of same-sized paper and use a paper cutter to cut square inches. When children's collages are dry, display them on a bulletin board for a One-Inch Art Gallery. Encourage children to share and compare their work.

One-Inch Art

Directions

① Choose a bag of paper. Use the squares in the bag to measure something in the classroom.

② Arrange the squares on a sheet of paper to make a collage model of the object you measured. Write your measurement on the paper.

③ Glue the paper in place. Use the crayons to add details to your collage.

④ Repeat steps 1 through 3 with a new object.

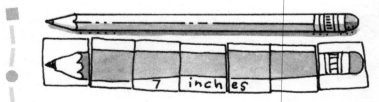

7 inches

Shoe Box Learning Centers: Time & Measurement   Scholastic Teaching Resources

Inchworm, Inchworm

In this game, children use inchworms to measure a variety of leaves.

Materials

- shoe box
- box label
- student directions
- scissors
- glue
- inchworm patterns (page 46)
- leaves of different lengths (or leaf patterns, page 46)
- paper bag
- resealable plastic bags

Shoe Box Setup

Copy the inchworms onto heavy green construction paper or card stock and cut them out. Place sets of inchworms in resealable bags. Collect leaves, making sure you have a variety of types and lengths. (If natural leaves are unavailable, make several copies of the leaf patterns and cut them out.) Place the leaves in a paper bag. Place the inchworm bags and leaf bag in the shoe box. Glue the label to one end of the box and the student directions to the inside of the lid.

TIP Introduce this shoe box center by sharing Leo Lionni's classic *Inch by Inch* (Astor-Honor, 1960). In this story, a resourceful inchworm measures different birds. As a variation, invite children to play the game with craft feathers instead of leaves.

Measuring Length

Inchworm, Inchworm

Directions
(for 2 players)

1. Each player takes a bag of inchworms.

2. Each player chooses a leaf from the bag. No peeking!

3. Let the worms crawl from one end of the leaf to the other by laying them on the leaf end to end.

4. Repeat with two more leaves. Count all the inchworms. Which player used the most worms all together?

5. Choose new leaves and play again.

Inchworm, Inchworm

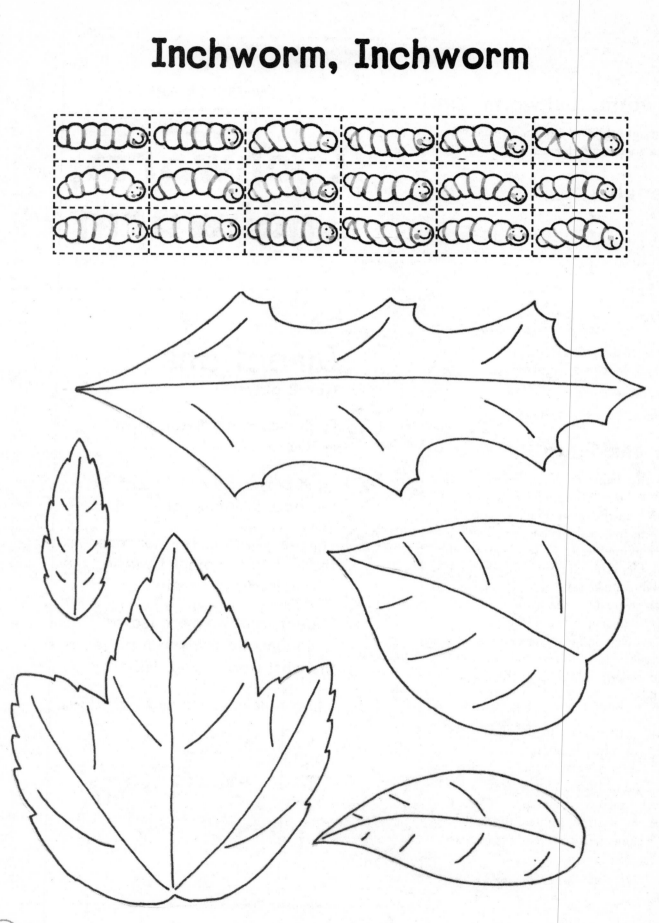

To Grandmother's House We Go

Children practice measuring distances as Little Red Riding Hood follows different paths to get to Grandma's house.

Materials

- shoe box
- box label
- student directions
- scissors
- glue
- story map (page 48)
- story cards (page 49)
- counters (such as dried beans or small math cubes)
- resealable plastic bags
- paper
- pencils

Shoe Box Setup

Copy the story map and story cards. Place counters in the resealable bags. Place the story maps, story cards, counters, paper, and pencils in the shoe box. Glue the label to one end of the box and the student directions to the inside of the lid.

TIP For a greater challenge, create more complex paths for students to take. You can write your own stories on index cards, including more stops on Little Red Riding Hood's path. You might also like to create stories for her return trip!

Measuring Length

To Grandmother's House We Go

Directions

1. Choose a story card.

2. Follow the story to make a path from Little Red Riding Hood's house to Grandma's house. Use counters to show the path.

3. How many counters did you use? Write the story card number and the number of counters on a sheet of paper.

4. Choose a new story card. Find out how many counters long the new path is. Which path is shorter?

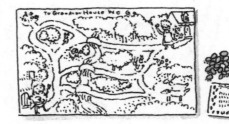

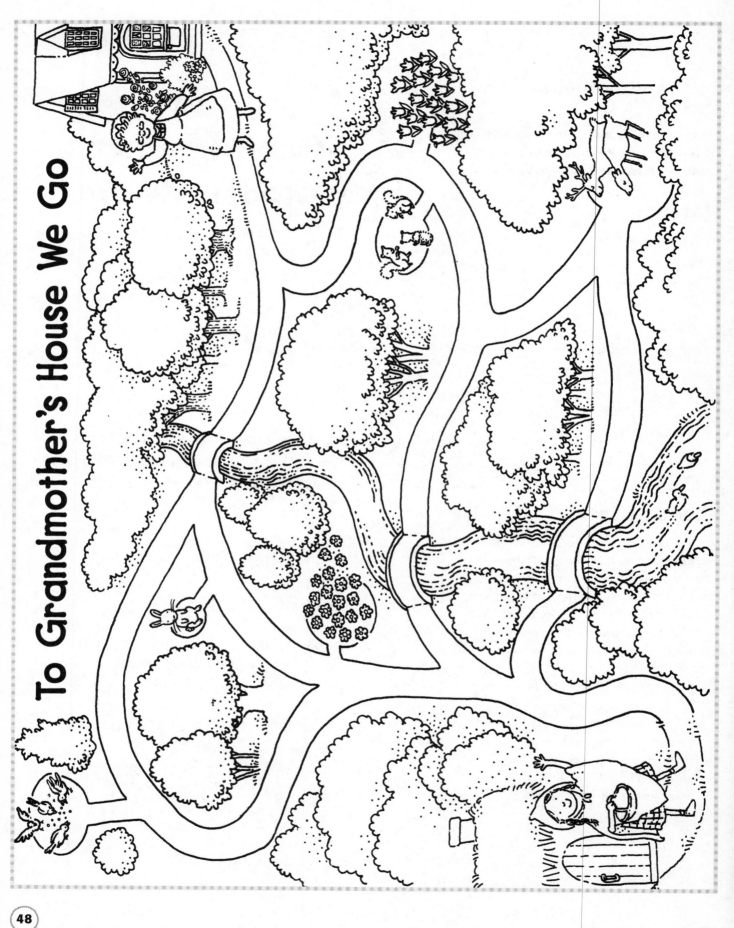

To Grandmother's House We Go

To Grandmother's House We Go

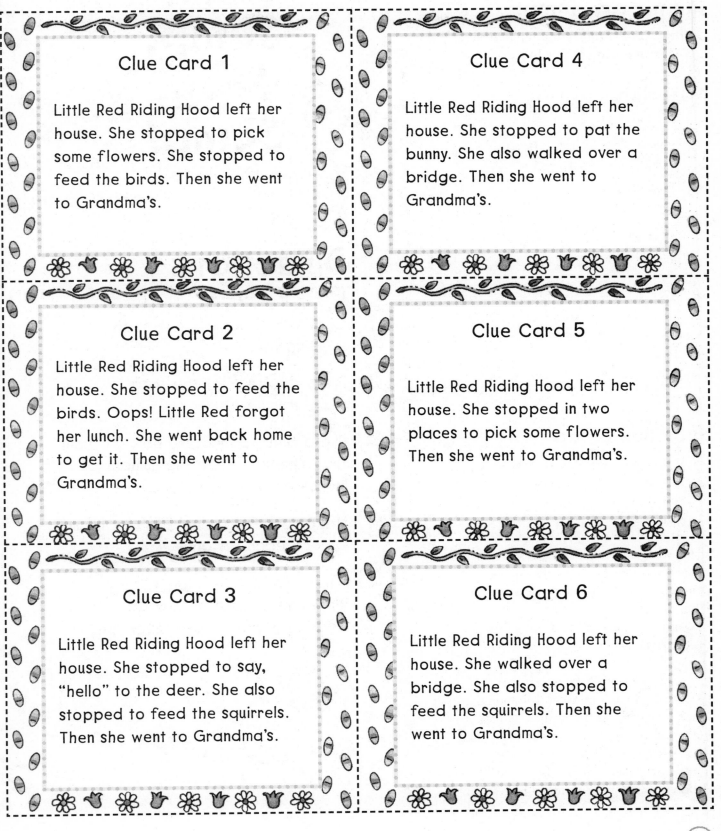

Clue Card 1

Little Red Riding Hood left her house. She stopped to pick some flowers. She stopped to feed the birds. Then she went to Grandma's.

Clue Card 4

Little Red Riding Hood left her house. She stopped to pat the bunny. She also walked over a bridge. Then she went to Grandma's.

Clue Card 2

Little Red Riding Hood left her house. She stopped to feed the birds. Oops! Little Red forgot her lunch. She went back home to get it. Then she went to Grandma's.

Clue Card 5

Little Red Riding Hood left her house. She stopped in two places to pick some flowers. Then she went to Grandma's.

Clue Card 3

Little Red Riding Hood left her house. She stopped to say, "hello" to the deer. She also stopped to feed the squirrels. Then she went to Grandma's.

Clue Card 6

Little Red Riding Hood left her house. She walked over a bridge. She also stopped to feed the squirrels. Then she went to Grandma's.

Jump, Frog, Jump!

Children enter a frog-jumping contest
and measure distance to win a prize.

Materials

- shoe box
- box label
- student directions
- scissors
- glue
- masking tape
- prize ribbons (page 51)
- yarn
- plastic jumping frogs (available at
  variety and toy stores; or at
  www.orientaltrading.com)
- rulers
- pencils
- paper

Shoe Box Setup

Set aside an area on the floor for the
frog-jumping contest. Use a strip of
masking tape to mark the starting line.
Copy and cut out the prize ribbons.
Punch a hole in the top of each, and
string with yarn to make a necklace.
Place the prize ribbons, frogs, rulers,
pencils, and paper in the shoe box.
Glue the label to one end of the
box and the student directions to the
inside of the lid.

 Show children how to
measure their frogs' jumps
with a 12-inch ruler, adding up
inches as they go. You can also provide
them with a yardstick or measuring tape
for practice with other tools. Invite
children to record their measurements in
feet and inches.

Jump, Frog, Jump!

Directions
(for 1–3 players)

1. Choose a frog. Place it on the
starting line.

2. Press the back of the frog to
make it jump.

3. Use a ruler to measure how far your
frog jumped. Write the number of
inches on a sheet of paper.

4. Make your frog jump 10 times in all.
Record each distance.

5. What is your frog's longest jump?
Write the number on a prize ribbon.
Wear your ribbon as a necklace!

Jump, Frog, Jump!

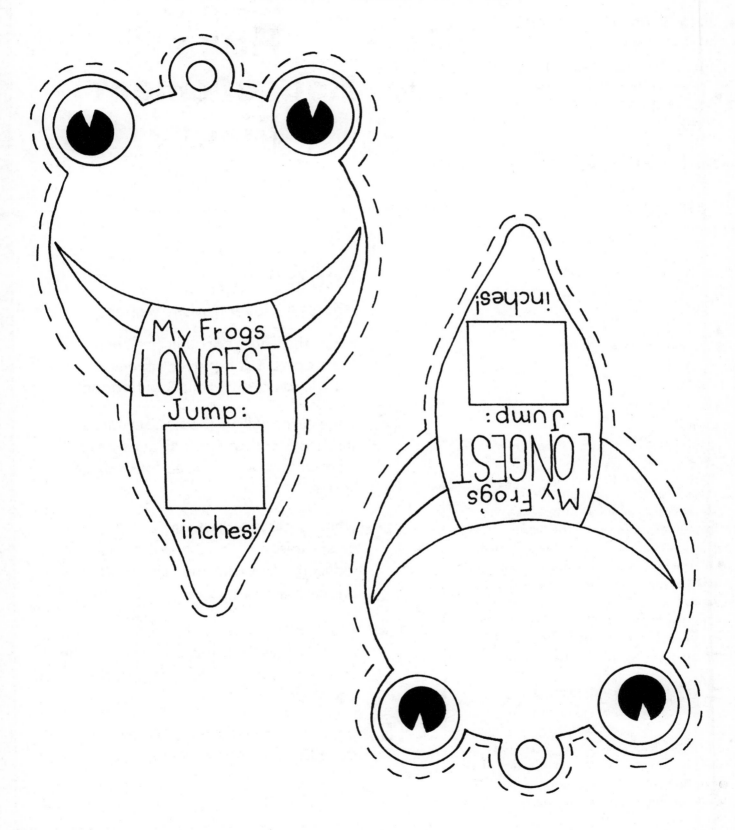

My Frog's
LONGEST
Jump:

inches!

Max's Measurement Diner

Children measure in inch and half-inch increments when they visit a diner that requires customers to measure their orders!

Materials

- shoe box
- box label
- student directions
- scissors
- glue
- game board (page 53)
- food cards (page 54)
- game markers and menu (page 55)
- tape
- number cube
- ruler

Shoe Box Setup

Copy the game board, food cards, game markers, and menu onto card stock and cut apart. To create the markers, fold in half along the center solid line, then fold the tabs under and tape together to make a base. Place the game board, game markers, food cards, menu, number cube, and ruler in the shoe box. Glue the label to one end of the box and the student directions to the inside of the lid.

TIP You can expand the game by creating new foods to add to the menu. Draw simple pictures on construction paper, or cut out pictures of foods from magazines. Add the names of the new foods and their measurements to the menu.

Measuring Length

Max's Measurement Diner

Directions
(for 3–4 players, plus "waiter")

1. Place the food cards in the center of the board. Each player places a marker on a different Start space.

2. Take turns rolling the number cube and moving that many spaces on the board. Follow any directions on the space.

3. When a player lands on "Eat Up!" he or she picks a food card, measures along the line with the ruler, and says the measurement.

4. The "waiter" checks the measurement on the menu. If the player is right, he or she keeps the card. If not, the card is put back.

5. Continue until all the cards are gone. The player with the most cards wins.

Max's Measurement Diner
Game Board

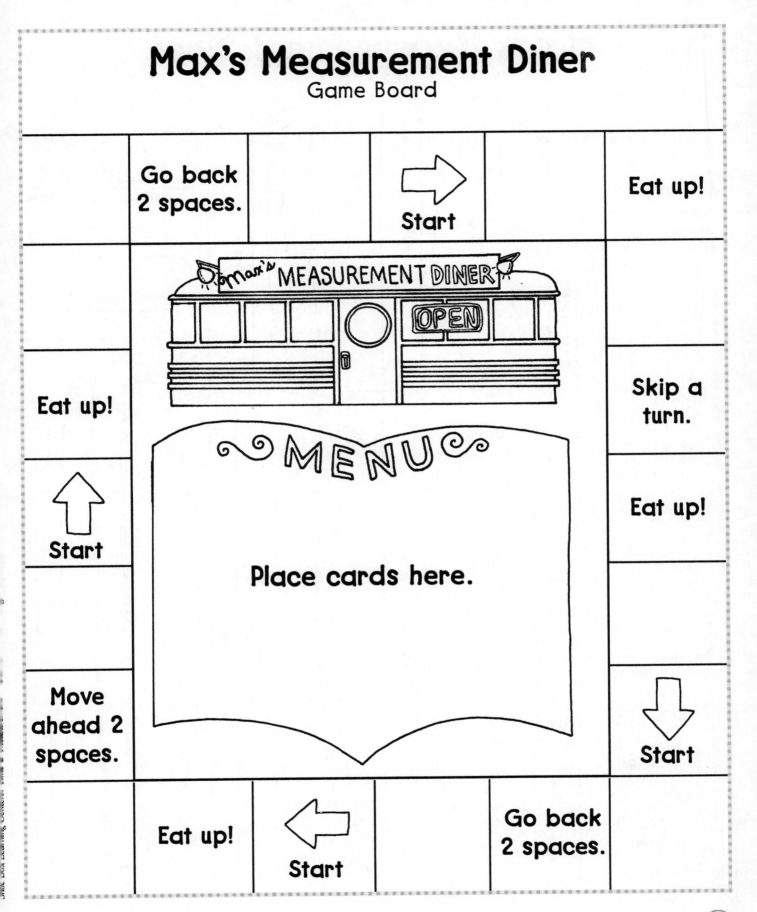

Go back 2 spaces.

Start

Eat up!

Max's MEASUREMENT DINER

OPEN

Eat up!

Skip a turn.

Start

Eat up!

MENU

Place cards here.

Move ahead 2 spaces.

Start

Eat up!

Start

Go back 2 spaces.

Max's Measurement Diner
Food Cards

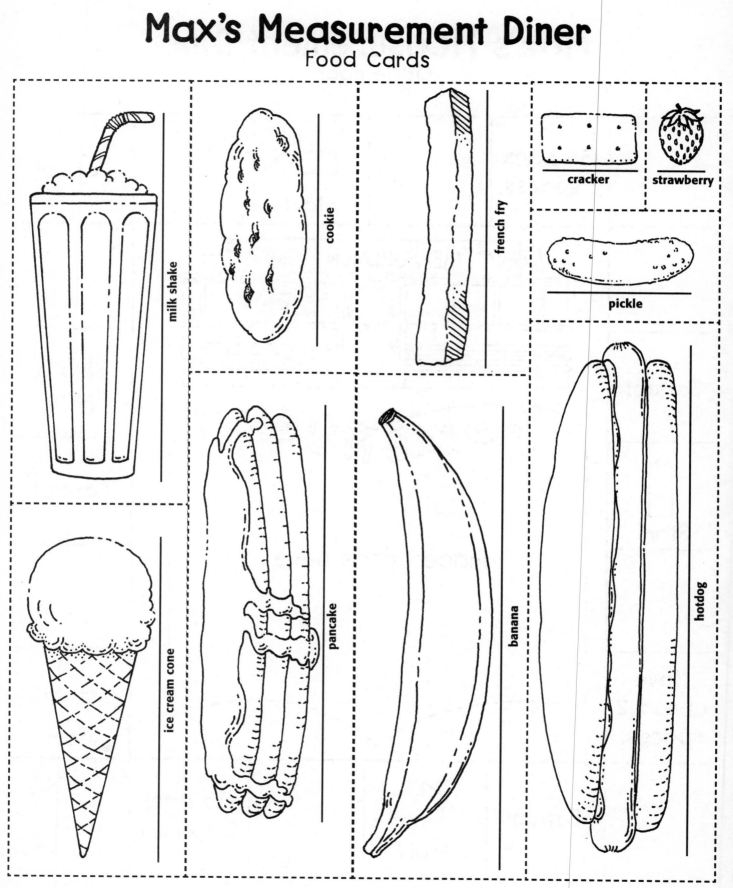

milk shake

cookie

french fry

cracker

strawberry

pickle

ice cream cone

pancake

banana

hotdog

Max's Measurement Diner
Game Markers and Menu

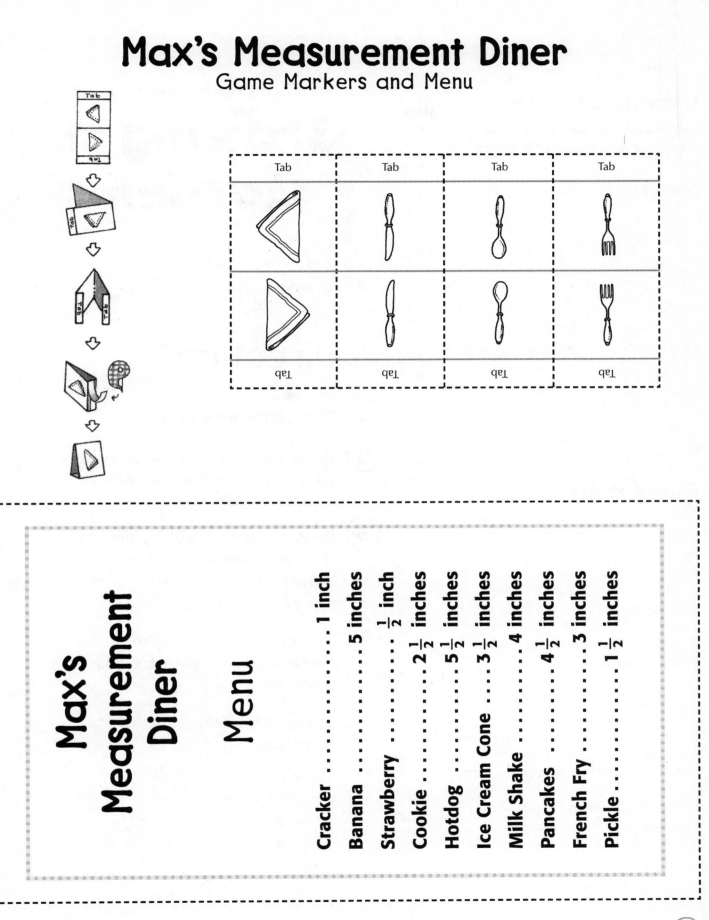

Tab	Tab	Tab	Tab
Tab	Tab	Tab	Tab

Max's Measurement Diner Menu

Cracker	1 inch
Banana	5 inches
Strawberry	$\frac{1}{2}$ inch
Cookie	$2\frac{1}{2}$ inches
Hotdog	$5\frac{1}{2}$ inches
Ice Cream Cone	$3\frac{1}{2}$ inches
Milk Shake	4 inches
Pancakes	$4\frac{1}{2}$ inches
French Fry	3 inches
Pickle	$1\frac{1}{2}$ inches

Side Box Learning Centers: Time & Measurement · Scholastic Teaching Resources

Growing a Garden

Children measure with seeds to see how many they need to "grow" a garden.

Materials

- shoe box
- box label
- student directions
- scissors
- glue
- flower patterns (page 57)
- craft sticks cut to different lengths
- green paint
- unshelled sunflower seeds (in a container)
- pencils
- paper

Shoe Box Setup

Make several copies of the flower patterns. Color, cut out, and laminate the flowers. Cut craft sticks to different lengths. Paint them green. Glue a flower top to each stick. Place the flowers, seeds, pencils, and paper in the shoe box. Glue the label to one end of the box and the student directions to the inside of the lid.

TIP **E**xtend this activity by providing two varieties of seeds, such as sunflower seeds and bean or pea seeds. Challenge children to grow the same garden with different seeds (for example, sunflower seeds and kidney bean seeds). They can base their estimations on the size of each seed.

Measuring Height

Growing a Garden

Directions

(1) Choose three flowers.

(2) Guess how many seeds tall each flower is. Write your guesses on a sheet of paper.

(3) Measure each flower by placing the seeds end to end. Start at the bottom of the stem. Stop at the top of the flower.

(4) Count how many seeds tall each flower is. How close were your guesses?

(5) Choose three new flowers. Grow a new garden.

Growing a Garden

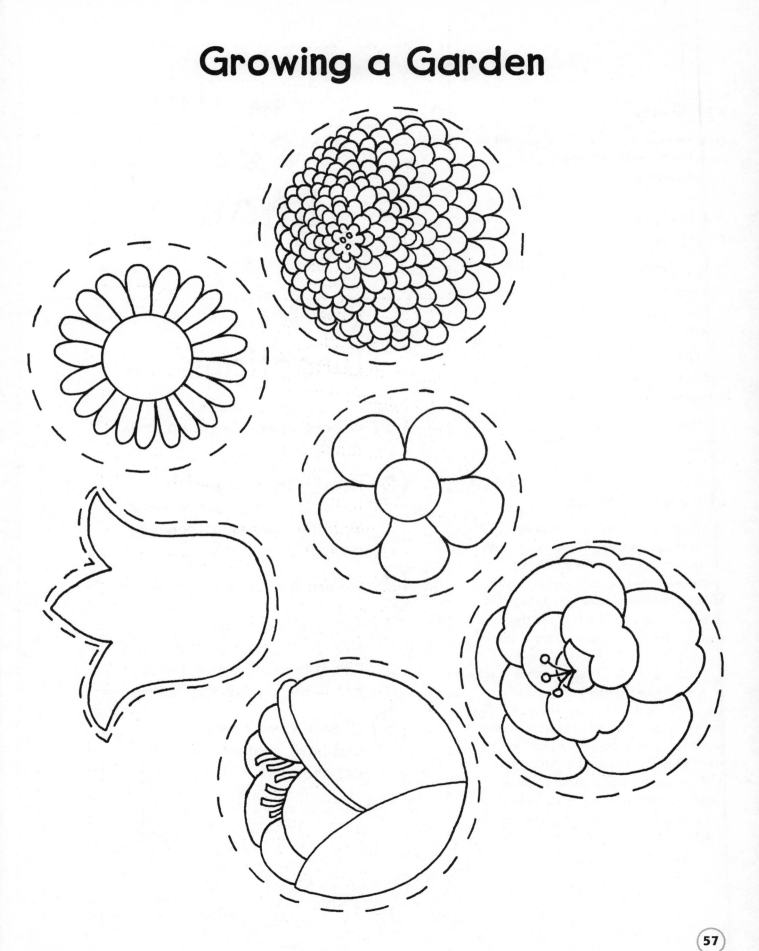

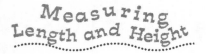

Pet Show

Children have a pet show and present an award to the pets with the largest measurements.

Materials

- shoe box
- box label
- student directions
- scissors
- glue
- pet trophies (page 59)
- toy animals
- rulers
- paper
- pencils
- crayons

Shoe Box Setup

Make copies of the pet trophies. Gather a variety of plastic or plush animals of different sizes. Place the trophies, animals, rulers, paper, pencils, and crayons in the shoe box. Glue the label to one end of the box and the student directions to the inside of the lid.

TIP **I**ntroduce this shoe box center by sharing Loreen Leedy's *Measuring Penny* (Holt, 1998). In this story, a girl measures her pet dog in many creative ways for a homework assignment. Invite children to suggest different body parts to measure (ears, tails) and measuring tools to use (dog biscuits, cotton swabs). Children can also weigh their "pets" on a balance scale.

Measuring Length and Height

Pet Show

Directions

1 Choose three pets to enter in a pet show.

2 Measure the first pet. Use a ruler to see how long and how tall. Write the number of inches on a sheet of paper.

3 Repeat step 2 for each pet.

4 Give the tallest pet an award. Give the longest pet an award. Fill in the blank to tell the kind of pet. Write the winning measurement.

5 Choose three new pets and have another pet show.

Pet Show

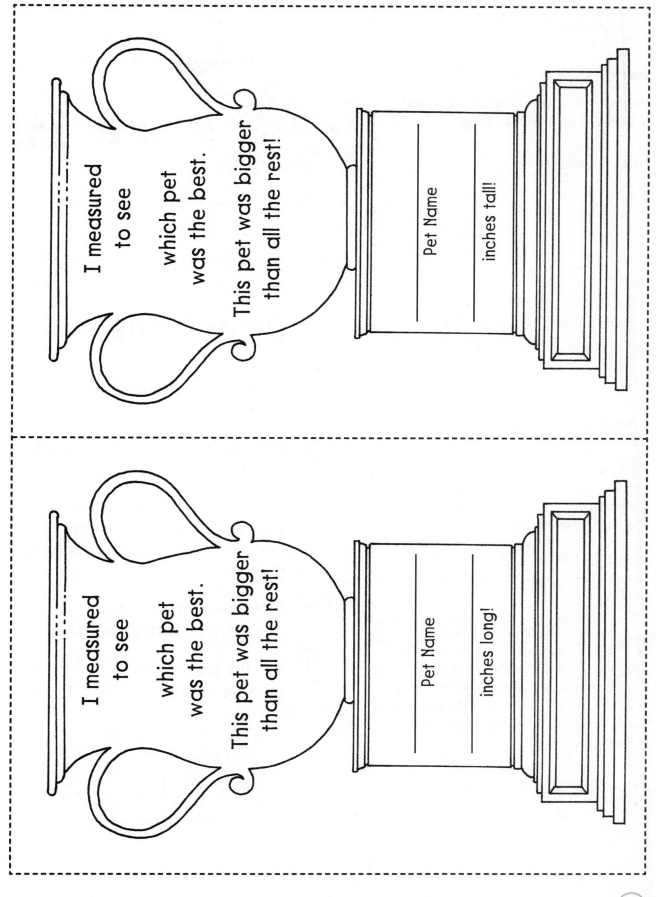

I measured
to see
which pet
was the best.

This pet was bigger
than all the rest!

Pet Name

_____ inches tall!

I measured
to see
which pet
was the best.

This pet was bigger
than all the rest!

Pet Name

_____ inches long!

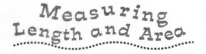
Park It!

Children follow an architect's "blueprint" to park cars on a lot they design.

Materials

- shoe box
- box label
- student directions
- scissors
- glue
- parking lot template (page 61)
- blueprint cards (page 62)
- toy vehicles of various sizes
- rulers
- crayons

Shoe Box Setup

Make copies of the parking lot template and blueprint cards. Cut out the cards. Collect toy vehicles of different sizes. Place the parking lot sheets, blueprint cards, vehicles, rulers, and crayons in the shoe box. Glue the label to one end of the box and the student directions to the inside of the lid.

TIP For a simplified activity on area, have children sort the toy vehicles into piles by size. Invite children to guess how many cars of each size will fit on the lot and then "park" them according to a blueprint to find out.

Measuring Length and Area

Park It!

Directions

1. Take a parking lot sheet. Choose a blueprint card.

2. Place a car on the lot. Draw lines to show the parking space.

3. Follow the blueprint to draw more parking spaces for more cars. Use a ruler to measure and mark the space between each car.

4. Park the cars on your lot. How many cars did you fit?

5. Use the blank card to make your own parking lot blueprint. Try it out.

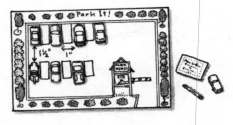

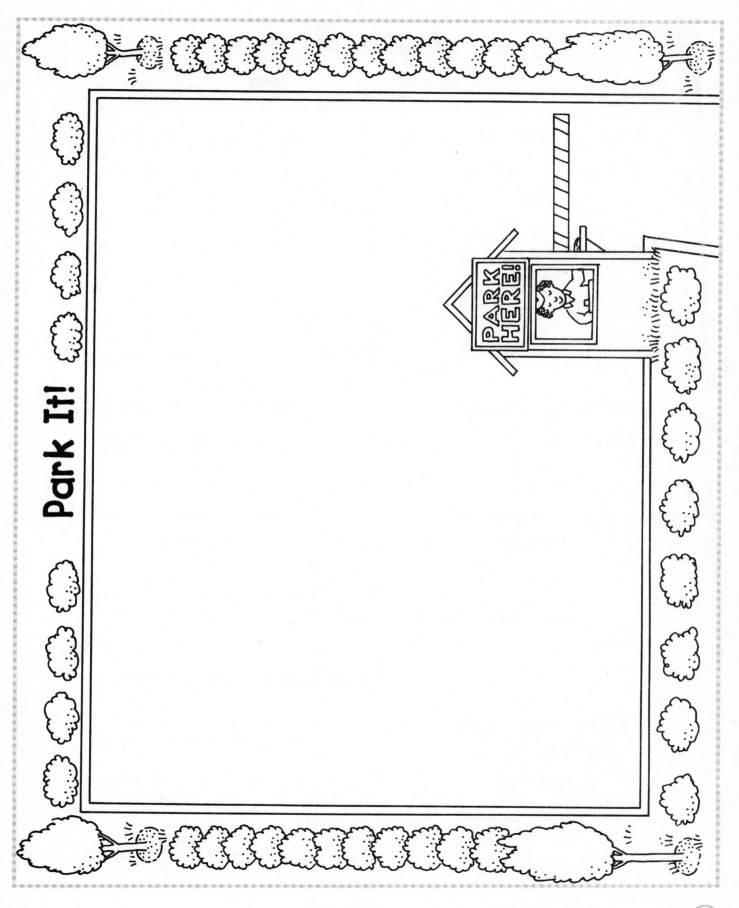

Park It!

PARK HERE!

Park It!

Parking Lot Blueprint

Space between each car:
1 inch

Space between each row:
1 inch

Parking Lot Blueprint

Space between each car:
$1\frac{1}{2}$ inches

Space between each row:
1 inch

Parking Lot Blueprint

Space between each car:
1 inch

Space between each row:
$1\frac{1}{2}$ inches

Parking Lot Blueprint

Space between each car:
$1\frac{1}{2}$ inches

Space between each row:
$1\frac{1}{2}$ inches

Make Your Own Parking Lot Blueprint

Space between each car:

_____

Space between each row:

_____

Shoe Box Learning Centers: Time & Measurement   Scholastic Teaching Resources

The Great Gack Olympics

Children perform great feats with "gack" and measure their results to win an award!

Materials

- shoe box
- box label
- student directions
- scissors
- glue
- event cards and certificates (page 64)
- gack (stretch play putty)
- plastic eggs
- rulers
- yarn
- pencils
- paper

Shoe Box Setup

Copy the event cards and certificates. Place handfuls of play putty in separate eggs, using the same amount for each. Cut yarn into one-foot lengths. Place the event cards, certificates, putty, rulers, yarn, pencils, and paper in the shoe box. Glue the label to one end of the box and the student directions to the inside of the lid.

TIP Commercial play putty may work best for this activity, but you can also make your own. Mix one part liquid starch and one part white glue. Add food coloring if you like. Let dry a bit until workable. Add more starch or glue as needed until you get the desired consistency. Store in an airtight container.

 Great Gack Olympics

Measuring Length and Perimeter

The Great Gack Olympics

Directions
(for 1–3 players)

(1) Choose an event card.

(2) All players follow the instructions for the event. Record your measurements on paper.

(3) Repeat the event three times. Circle your best score.

(4) Win your award! Write the name of the event and your best score.

(5) Choose a new event and play again.

The Great Gack Olympics

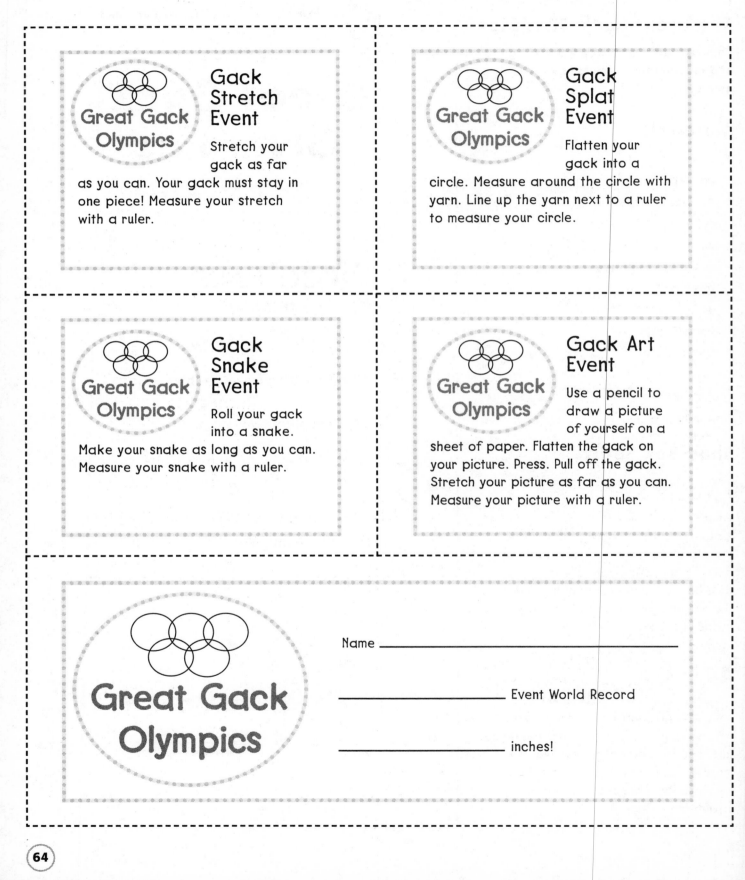

Gack Stretch Event

Stretch your gack as far as you can. Your gack must stay in one piece! Measure your stretch with a ruler.

Gack Splat Event

Flatten your gack into a circle. Measure around the circle with yarn. Line up the yarn next to a ruler to measure your circle.

Gack Snake Event

Roll your gack into a snake. Make your snake as long as you can. Measure your snake with a ruler.

Gack Art Event

Use a pencil to draw a picture of yourself on a sheet of paper. Flatten the gack on your picture. Press. Pull off the gack. Stretch your picture as far as you can. Measure your picture with a ruler.

Great Gack Olympics

Name _____

_____ Event World Record

_____ inches!

Shoe Box Learning Centers: Time & Measurement   Scholastic Teaching Resources

Pizza, Please!

Children explore area as they top pizzas with favorite fixin's!

Materials

- shoe box
- box label
- student directions
- scissors
- glue
- pizza patterns (page 66)
- pizza menu sheets (page 67)
- pizza "toppings" (such as buttons, bingo markers, dried beans)
- resealable plastic bags
- pencils

Shoe Box Setup

Copy the pizza patterns onto card stock and cut them out. Make several copies of the pizza menu sheet. Place each "topping" in a separate resealable bag. Label each bag with a topping name (such as pepperoni, meatballs, and sausage). Place the pizzas, menu sheets, bag of toppings, and pencils in the shoe box. Glue the label to one end of the box and the student directions to the inside of the lid.

TIP To incorporate fractions, have students estimate and count how many toppings will fit on half a pizza, a quarter of a pizza, an eighth of a pizza, and so on.

Measuring Area

Pizza, Please!

Directions

1. Take a menu. Place the small pizza in front of you. Choose a topping.

2. How many pieces will fit on your pizza? Write your guess on the menu.

3. Place the toppings on your pizza until it is full. Make sure all the pieces touch without overlapping.

4. Count the pieces and write the number.

5. Repeat with the medium and large pizzas.

6. Choose a new topping and try it again.

Pizza, Please!

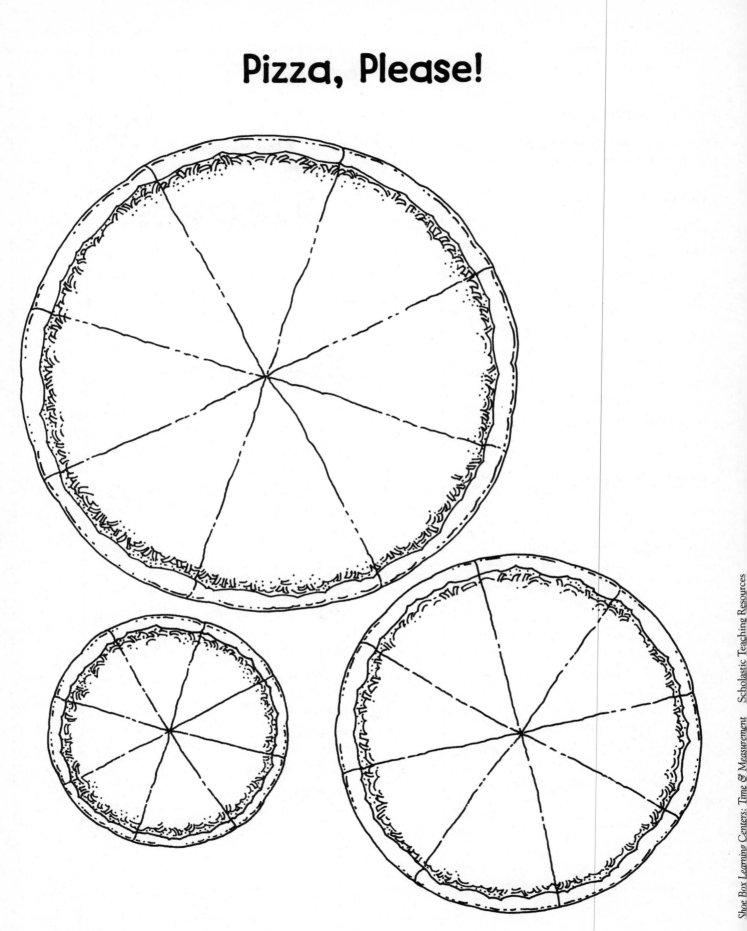

Shoe Box Learning Centers: Time & Measurement   Scholastic Teaching Resources

Pizza, Please!

Name_____ Date _____

Small Pizza Menu

Pizza Topping	My Guess	How Many Pieces?
Topping 1		
Topping 2		
Topping 3		

Medium Pizza Menu

Pizza Topping	My Guess	How Many Pieces?
Topping 1		
Topping 2		
Topping 3		

Large Pizza Menu

Pizza Topping	My Guess	How Many Pieces?
Topping 1		
Topping 2		
Topping 3		

Measuring Area

Build a Skyline

Children explore the concept of area as they roll number cubes to build a city with a centimeter grid.

Materials

- shoe box
- box label
- student directions
- scissors
- glue
- centimeter grid (page 69)
- number cubes
- pencils
- paper
- crayons and markers

Shoe Box Setup

Make several copies of the centimeter grid. Place them in the shoe box along with two number cubes for each child, pencils, paper, crayons, markers, glue, and scissors. Glue the label to one end of the box and the student directions to the inside of the lid.

TIP To make mathematical comparisons, display children's skylines next to one another in a row. Challenge children to count the squares to figure out which buildings have the largest area. Which have the same area? Do these buildings have to have the same height and width or can they be different? Let children use linking cubes or blocks to create their buildings on a larger scale.

Measuring Area

Build a Skyline

Directions
(for 2 players)

 1 Roll the number cube two times. Write the numbers on your paper. Use the higher number for the height of your first building. Use the lower number for the width.

 2 Color in squares on the grid to match the numbers you rolled.

 3 Roll the number cubes again to plan your next building. Color in squares to make this building.

 4 Keep rolling and coloring to make as many buildings as you can with your squares. You can use a different color for each building.

 5 Cut out each building. Glue your buildings to a sheet of paper to make a city. Draw other things that you see in your city.

Build a Skyline

To Market, to Market

Children go "shopping" to see whose grocery bag holds the most weight!

Materials

- shoe box
- box label
- student directions
- scissors
- glue
- shopping lists (page 71)
- balance scale
- groceries (3 cans of soup, 5 single-serving boxes of cereal, 3 small juice boxes, 5 small cans of cat food, 7 snack-size boxes of raisins)
- paper lunch bags

Shoe Box Setup

Copy the shopping lists and cut them apart. Place a balance scale in the center. Place the shopping lists, groceries, and paper bags in the shoe box. Glue the label to one end of the box and the student directions to the inside of the lid.

TIP Expand students' investigations with weight by creating new shopping lists. If you have play food in the classroom, include those items on shopping lists. Children might also enjoy creating play produce to add to the lists. Provide them with colored clay and have them create bananas, oranges, pears, carrots, and other fruits and vegetables.

Measuring Weight

To Market, to Market

Directions
(for 2 players)

1. Each player chooses a shopping list.

2. Read your lists. Guess whose groceries will weigh more.

3. Now go shopping! Place each item on your list in a bag.

4. Place the bags on the balance scale. Which groceries weigh more?

5. Choose two new lists and play again.

Shoe Box Learning Centers: Time & Measurement   Scholastic Teaching Resources

To Market, to Market

Shopping List 1

1 can cat food

1 box cereal

1 juice box

Shopping List 2

2 juice boxes

1 box raisins

1 box cereal

Shopping List 3

1 can soup

1 can cat food

2 boxes raisins

Shopping List 4

1 can soup

2 boxes cereal

1 box raisins

Shopping List 5

2 boxes raisins

1 box cereal

1 can cat food

Shopping List 6

1 box raisins

1 can soup

2 cans cat food

Measuring Volume

Three Bears Fill Their Bowls

Children investigate volume by seeing how much of different foods will fill each of the three bears' bowls.

Materials

- shoe box
- box label
- student directions
- scissors
- glue
- record sheet (page 73)
- three bowls (small, medium, and large)
- cereal (such as O-shaped rings), uncooked rice, uncooked elbow noodles
- resealable plastic bags
- teaspoons
- pencils

Shoe Box Setup

Before copying the record sheet, write in a food, such as O-shaped cereal, that students will measure. Make a record sheet for each food that you include. Measure out enough of each food to fill all three bowls. Include a little extra of each. Place each food in a plastic bag and seal. Place record sheets, bowls, food bags, teaspoons, and pencils in the shoe box. Glue the label to one end of the box and the student directions to the inside of the lid.

TIP **T**o build counting and addition skills, have children calculate how many spoonfuls of each food all together fill the three bowls. Or challenge children to guess and then find out if a specified number of spoonfuls of a food (such as the dried beans) will fill all three bowls.

Measuring Volume

Three Bears Fill Their Bowls

Directions

① Place the bowls in front of you.

② Take a record sheet. Select a bag of food.

③ Look at the food. Guess how many teaspoons of this food will fill Little Bear's bowl. Write that number on your record sheet. Do the same for Mama Bear's and Papa Bear's bowl.

④ Measure to see how many teaspoons of the food will fit in each bowl. Write these numbers on your record sheet.

⑤ Repeat with a new food.

Name _____ Date _____

Three Bears Fill Their Bowls

Food_____	Estimate	Measurement
Little Bear's Bowl	_____ teaspoons	_____ teaspoons
Mama Bear's Bowl	_____ teaspoons	_____ teaspoons
Papa Bear's Bowl	_____ teaspoons	_____ teaspoons

Name _____ Date _____

Three Bears Fill Their Bowls

Food_____	Estimate	Measurement
Little Bear's Bowl	_____ teaspoons	_____ teaspoons
Mama Bear's Bowl	_____ teaspoons	_____ teaspoons
Papa Bear's Bowl	_____ teaspoons	_____ teaspoons

The Old Woman Who Lived in a Shoe

Children explore volume with a favorite nursery rhyme.

Materials

- shoe box
- box label
- student directions
- scissors
- glue
- record sheet (page 75)
- shoes (different sizes)
- small objects (such as counting bears, blocks, clothespins, and uncooked bow-tie noodles)
- resealable plastic bags
- pencils

Shoe Box Setup

Copy the record sheets. Collect a variety of old shoes in different sizes, such as baby shoes, a child-size sneaker, and an adult loafer. Remove any laces to make shoes easier to fill. Collect a variety of shoe-filling items (any item of uniform size will work). Place a number of each item in a separate resealable bag. Place the record sheets, bags, pencils, and shoes in the shoe box. Glue the label to one end of the box and the student directions to the inside of the lid.

 TIP You may want to place one shoe in the shoe box at a time and rotate each week. Or place two shoes of different sizes in the shoe box at once. Invite children to use the same item to fill each shoe, using the size of each shoe to help make estimates.

Measuring Volume

The Old Woman Who Lived in a Shoe

Directions

1. Take a shoe. Choose an item to fill the shoe.

2. Take a shoe sheet. Write the name of the item in the first two spaces

3. How many will fit in the shoe? Write your guess. Then fill the shoe to the top.

4. Empty the shoe and count the items. Write your answer.

5. Read the rhyme!

6. Choose a new item and repeat.

The Old Woman Who Lived in a Shoe

There was
an old woman
who lived in a shoe.

She had so many

_____

she didn't know
what to do!

How many

_____

will fit in her shoe?

My Guess:_____

My Answer:_____

Measuring Mini-Books

Children create a book to show which tools they can use to make different kinds of measurements.

Materials

- shoe box
- box label
- student directions
- scissors
- glue
- mini-book pages (pages 77–78)
- mini-book pictures (page 78)
- paper
- crayons

Shoe Box Setup

Make copies of the mini-book pages and pictures. Cut apart the book pages, place them in order, add a cover, and staple them together. Place the mini-books, pictures, crayons, scissors, and glue in the shoe box. Glue the label to one end of the box and the student directions to the inside of the lid.

TIP **Y**ou can expand children's mini-books by adding blank pages. Invite children to draw more things they'd like to measure, and have them write the names for and draw pictures of the tools they would use. Once children's books are complete, invite them to share their books with partners. Encourage them to discuss different ways they could use each tool and measure each item.

Choosing Appropriate Measuring Tools

Measuring Mini-Books

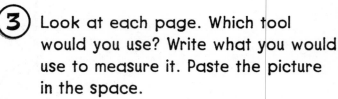

Directions

1 Write your name on the cover.

2 Cut out the measuring tool pictures. You can color them in if you like.

3 Look at each page. Which tool would you use? Write what you would use to measure it. Paste the picture in the space.

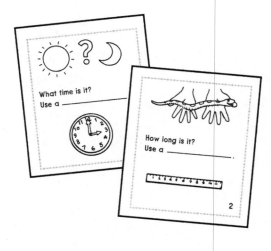

Measuring Mini-Books

What time is it?

Use a _____.

1

How cold is it outside?

Use a _____.

3

How long is it?

Use a _____.

2

How much does it hold?

Use a _____.

4

Measuring Mini-Books

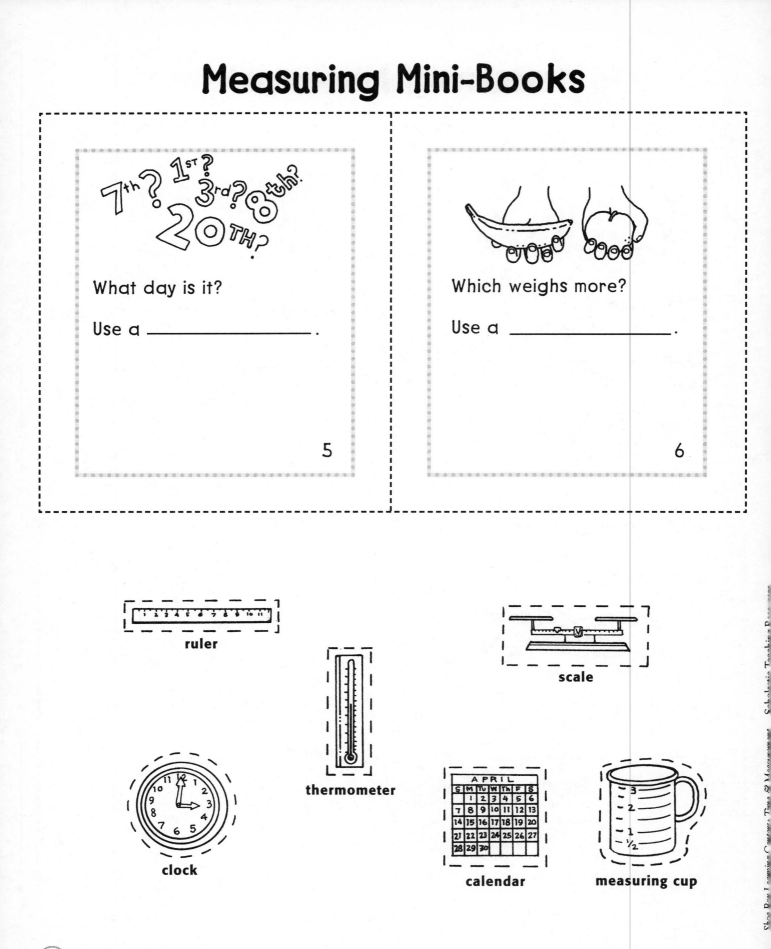

What day is it?

Use a _____.

5

Which weighs more?

Use a _____.

6

ruler

scale

thermometer

clock

calendar

measuring cup

More Easy-to-Make Shoe Box Learning Centers

Add to your supply of shoe box centers periodically by creating fresh activities to keep student interest strong. Following are more ideas for making shoe box centers that reinforce counting skills. For each, use the reproducible templates (right) to make a label and write student directions. Glue the label to one end of the box and the student directions to the inside of the lid.

What Time Is It?

Children practice telling time as they make clock collages.

Stock a shoe box with pictures from magazines and advertisements that show clocks and watches. Also provide scissors, glue, paper, pencils, and markers. Have children cut out pictures of clocks and watches from the print material and use them to make a collage. Ask them to record the time (or just the hour for a simpler exercise) next to each picture. Use the pictures to help students learn more about the features of clocks and watches. Students can classify pictures by these features— for example, sorting by those that show hands and those that don't and those that have numbers and those that don't.

Directions

Five-Minute Alarm

Teach concepts of time with a center that also strengthens estimation and reading skills.

Place an alarm clock or timer in a shoe box, along with sticky notes and several picture books about time. Have children choose a book to read and place a sticky note on the page they think they can read to in five minutes. Have them set the alarm or timer for five minutes and then read. When the alarm goes off, have children check to see how close they came to their estimates. They can set the alarm or timer and try again. As a variation, try 10, 15, or 20 minutes. Encourage children to make reasonable estimates.

Match That Measurement

Children learn about selecting appropriate units and tools for the attributes being measured with an easy-to-make matching game.

Glue pictures of various measuring tools (such as a ruler, yardstick, meter stick, tape measure, measuring cups, measuring spoons, and scales) on index cards. Glue pictures of objects that people might measure (such as a sheet of paper, a fence, a person, flour, apples or other produce, water, and salt) on index cards. Place the picture cards in the shoe box. Have children match the cards to show which tool they would use to measure each object. It's okay to match more than one object to a measuring tool. Periodically add new cards to the shoe box to provide more practice.

Is It or Isn't It?

Provide practice in estimating length with this fun guessing game.

Collect an assortment of small objects ranging from 1/2 inch long to about 10 inches long. Examples of objects are a rubber band, a stick of wrapped bubble gum, an envelope, a playing card, a toy car, connecting blocks (in different lengths), a small shoe, a paper clip, a CD case, a book, and a sponge. Place the objects in a brown bag. On index cards, write the length of each object (one per card). Place the objects, the

cards, and measuring tools in the shoe box. Have children shuffle the cards, place them facedown, and then randomly select an object and turn over the top card. Have children tell whether they think the measurement matches the object (and if not, is the object longer or shorter than the measurement on the card), and then measure to find out.

Craft-Stick Squares

Children build a square with craft sticks to explore measurements of area.

Place sets of four craft sticks in bags, one set per bag. Show students how to use the sticks to form a square (overlapping the ends at each corner). Stock the shoe box with the craft sticks, lots of small objects (such as bear counters, buttons, dried beans, and paper clips; each type of item stored in a separate bag), paper, and pencils. Have children use the sticks to form a square and then choose a type of object to place in the square. Ask children to estimate how many of each object will fit in the square and then fill the square to find out. To keep the center fresh, periodically rotate new objects into the shoe box. Students can experiment with using four rulers to form squares, too.

Mini-Muffin Makers

Children explore volume as they fill mini-muffin tins with different substances.

Place a mini-muffin tin (a toy tin with six sections is a good size, but a baking tin with 12 sections will work, too), baking cups, cup-size yogurt containers filled with various dry substances (such as sand, small uncooked noodles, dried beans, and flour), measuring spoons, paper, and pencils in a shoe box. Have children guess how much of each substance it will take to fill the muffin cups and then measure to find out. Have them record guesses and actual amounts and then compare.